Member of Parliament

The Job of a Backbencher

LISANNE RADICE

ELIZABETH VALLANCE

VIRGINIA WILLIS

Second Edition

M
MACMILLAN

First edition 1987
Reprinted 1988
Second edition 1990

Published by
THE MACMILLAN PRESS LTD
Houndmills, Basingstoke, Hampshire, RG21 2XS
and London
Companies and representatives
throughout the world

Printed in Hong Kong

British Library Cataloguing in Publication Data
Radice, Lisanne
Member of parliament: the job of a backbencher. — 2nd ed
1. Great Britain. Parliament. House of Commons.
Private members
I. Title II. Vallance, Elizabeth III. Willis, Virginia
328.41′0731
ISBN 0–333–49121–1 (hardcover)
ISBN 0–333–49122–X (paperback)

Please renew/return this item by the last date shown.

So that your telephone call is charged at local rate, please call the numbers as set out below:

	From Area codes 01923 or 0208:	From the rest of Herts:
Renewals:	01923 471373	01438 737373
Enquiries:	01923 471333	01438 737333
Minicom:	01923 471599	01438 737599

L32b   Checked 15/9/11

L32

30 APR 1994   1 3 MAR 1998   1 0 DEC 2002

0 4 FEB 1995   0 6 FEB 2002

0 7 NOV 1997

                    2 8 FEB 2002
                    2 8 MAR 2002
1 1 DEC 1999

                    2 6 APR 2002

To Giles, Iain and Brian

Contents

Acknowledgements

We should like to thank the many members of Parliament who talked to us in the course of our research for this book. We are particularly grateful to the MPs who gave us copies of their diaries – Angela Rumbold, Charles Wardle, Chris Smith, Roger Gale and Archy Kirkwood. Special thanks are due to Austin Mitchell MP, whose research for the All-Party Reform Group is much drawn upon here, Jenny Jeger for allowing us access to her 1974 research interviews, and to Giles Radice MP for his editorial advice. We are indebted to Geoffrey Lock, Jennifer Tanfield and all the staff of the House of Commons Library for their advice and the material they made available to us. Doug Jones of the Computer Centre of Brunel University helped us with the statistical data, Professor Trevor Smith kindly read and commented on early versions of several chapters, Ted Vallance patiently and meticulously compiled the index, and Jean and Bill McGonnigill helped with proof-reading. Finally, thanks to Anne-Marie Maggs, Yvonne South and Claire Gibling for their transcription of tapes and typing of scripts. In spite of all this support, the responsibility for any remaining errors of fact or presentation remains ours.

L.R.
E.V.
V.W.

List of Abbreviations

AGM	Annual General Meeting
CBI	Confederation of British Industry
col(s)	column(s)
DES	Department of Education and Science
DHSS	Department of Health and Social Security
EEC	European Economic Community
HC Deb.	*House of Commons Debates*
HMSO	Her Majesty's Stationery Office
MP	Member of Parliament
NOP	National Opinion Polls
ORC	Opinion Research Centre
plc	public limited company
PPS	Parliamentary Private Secretary
pr	public relations
SDP	Social Democratic Party
SLDP	Social and Liberal Democratic Party
TSRB	Top Salaries Review Body
TUC	Trades Union Congress

Introduction to the Second Edition

It is always gratifying for authors to be asked to prepare a second edition of a book. It normally indicates that the work has been kindly received and, most important for the publishers, sold well. We are pleased to have the opportunity to update, clarify and extend some of the arguments of the first edition.

The 1987 general election took place just before the first edition was published and, although there were no dramatic changes in the balance of power, we welcomed the opportunity to arrange another round of interviews with members of the new House. These concentrated mainly on MPs coming in for the first time in 1987 and were carried out during the summer of 1988. The results have been incorporated into the text.

Very soon after the election, the Alliance parties, the Liberals and the SDP, agreed to merge and form a single, new party. In 1988, the basic structure of this new entity, the Social and Liberal Democrats (SLD), was agreed, with a residual SDP remaining as a separate and dissenting group. All the Alliance members of the 1987 parliament were, however, elected under Liberal or SDP heads and we have generally continued to refer to them as such, with updating references to the SLD where appropriate.

In all other respects, we have attempted to give the most up-to-date facts and figures (on salaries, allowances, backgrounds, reforms etc) at the time of writing. If these do not all remain accurate, even for the life of one parliament, it is because the system is organic and so, in consequence, is the job of a back-bencher.

L.R.
E.V.
V.W.

Introduction to the First Edition

> *Not so much a job as a fascinating way of life.*
> (Andrew Mitchell MP)

This is not a book aimed primarily at the parliamentary specialist. It is a book for the interested general reader or student of Parliament who wants to know more about the backbench job in the House of Commons. We do not set out, therefore, to discuss the procedures of the House or the process of legislation, the role of Parliament or the intricacies of constitutional reform. Where these arise, they do so in the context of making clearer the role we seek to describe. We believe that the job of the MP, both in Parliament and in the constituency, has changed considerably in the last ten years as, for example, constituency pressures mounted, the new Select Committees got underway, and the volume of legislation constantly increased.

The students of Parliament, for whom we are writing, may also include many MPs who themselves admit to finding it difficult to discover exactly what their job is. As one remarked, 'there ought to be a new boys' induction course: it would have made my first six weeks in the House a lot less miserable'. Another admitted that the balance of the job had been a bit of a surprise to him as he had not known even of the existence of Commons Committees until he got to the House! The confusion is more than a result of simple ignorance of the geography of the Palace of Westminster, or the, sometimes arcane, procedures of the Commons. It is also often a result of the diffuse demands, perhaps not always obviously compatible, of the job itself. The ambitious, the fortunate and the able need not stay backbenchers for ever. For many the job is only a necessary way station to power in government or greater status and influence on the opposition front benches. Their progress is another story. Here we concentrate on backbenchers and the job they do, as members themselves see it and not as either the job others think they could be doing, or constitutionalists think they should be doing.

The book is therefore largely structured around two themes; the reality of the job of an MP and the job as perceived by the practitioners and others. Three main sources of information have been used: Parliamentary Papers, official reports and secondary sources relating to the work of MPs, either academic studies, or autobiographical/biographical works; a questionnaire sent out by the All-Party Reform Group to Members of Parliament in 1983 which had a 52 per cent response rate; and, finally, interviews with MPs as well as the monthly diaries of four backbenchers.

Chapter 1 deals with the public perception of the job of an MP. We argue that, although there is no 'job description' which prescribes the work of a backbencher, no particular qualifications needed, nor a specific daily routine required, nevertheless it is possible to identify some common tasks and objectives which all backbenchers share. Historically, much of the discussion on the role of MPs has centred on the question of whether they are delegates or representatives.

More recently, the emphasis has moved to the relationship of the MP to his local Party, the increase in the importance of constituency work, as well as the problems resulting from the sheer volume and complexity of modern legislation. These changes have produced an interesting dichotomy. On the one hand, in the Commons, MPs have had to become more specialised; on the other, they find that their constituents frequently regard them as glorified social workers who happen to spend some of their time at Westminster. Nor do the tensions end there, for in the heartlands of their constituencies members are treated with respect and attention; back at Westminster, they lose their sense of power and purpose in the boredom of toeing the Party line, joining the ranks of those (as polls invariably demonstrate) low in public esteem and uncertain of the nature of their calling.

There is no doubt that there have been recent changes in the types of people entering politics. Chapter 2 explores the background of those getting into Parliament, the selection process through which all hopeful aspirants have to pass, and the qualifications, formal and informal, necessary for the job. MPs, it is noted, mainly arrive in Parliament by one of two or three routes: through local government, the local Party, or, in the case of Labour MPs, the Trade Union movement. More members of all parties have a degree these days and Conservative MPs are now likely to have attended a grammar school rather than, as previously, the more famous public schools. Politics, too, is most often seen now as a full-time job and, it is hoped, a job for life. But in spite of all these changes, the Commons is still overwhelmingly male, white and middle-class.

The third chapter returns to an analysis of the problems which arise in producing a job description for an MP's work. We show that members are expected to perform so many tasks (for instance, being spokesman for local interests, ombudsman, legislator, a check on the executive, and contributor to the national debate) that they are expected to cultivate a formidable array of skills and talents. Not only this but, because of the variety of tasks with which they are presented, they produce their own job descriptions simply through the choices they make as to which roles they think are the most important.

What emerges is that MPs currently work over 60 hours a week and collectively keep the longest and latest hours of any Western Parliament; they seldom have a free weekend, and see little of their families. When the House is sitting, many backbenchers are on one or two Committees a week, attend daily Question Time in addition to numerous meetings both inside the House and out, and those with far-flung constituencies travel endlessly. Deluged by letters from constituents, their postbags also bulging with pressure-group circulars, they struggle towards their weekend constituency surgeries where local cases add to their burden. And if not all members are quite so overworked as this suggests, the description probably fits most of them some of the time and some of them all of the time. To illustrate the great variations possible in backbencher life at Westminster, we have produced, in Chapter 4, a fictitious day in the life of two MPs, one from the government, the other from the Opposition side. Various important facets of parliamentary life such as Debates, Standing Committees, Select Committees, Question Time, the Adjournment Debate, Early-Day Motions, and so on, are described from a backbench perspective.

British MPs are amongst the worst paid in Europe; they also have generally poor conditions of service and working environments. In Chapter 5 we discuss members' pay, allowances and conditions; for example, the level of secretarial assistance, research help, advice from Party headquarters and support from the staff of the Commons Library on which members can count. We also ask whether members feel that the notoriously bad accommodation inhibits their working effectively.

Chapter 6 deals with the job outside the House of Commons. We discuss time spent in the constituency and on Party business and then go on to suggest reasons why so many MPs have paid jobs outside Westminster (as consultants, company directors, lawyers and accountants, etc.). Despite their parliamentary duties and outside commitments, however, many MPs still claim to find time to pursue recreational activities, whether it is walking, going to the theatre, playing sports, bee-keeping, poodle breeding or simply reading. Some even write books. And most seem to keep at least Sunday free for communication with their families!

How do MPs see their job? And to what extent does this reality fit in with their original expectations? Chapter 7, based mainly on our own interviews and the All-Party Reform Group questionnaire, examines these questions. Different emphases tend to be laid by the different parties on the various roles of the parliamentarian. Conservative MPs often see themselves as mainly contributing to national debate; Labour politicians, on the other hand, tend to see their most important contribution as that of spokesman for local interests, while the Alliance members generally believe that keeping a check on the executive is the fundamental job. The majority of MPs appear reasonably satisfied with their work, although many find the extent of their constituency commitments too demanding and almost all agree that the accommodation at Westminster leaves much to be desired.

Chapter 8 provides four case-studies which illustrate something of the reality of backbench life, with the monthly diaries of four MPs illustrating the variety, excitement and also the banality of the backbencher's job. A cross-section of the Parties is provided, with two Tory MPs (to reflect the current very large Tory majority), one Labour and one Liberal. The Conservatives represent a suburban and a farming and seaside constituency; the Labour member has an Inner London constituency; and the Liberal, a far-flung constituency just north of the Scottish border. Although interests are different, as are the calls of the various constituencies, nevertheless a pattern does emerge – a life of constant change, little daily routine, and activity perhaps more ceaseless than productive.

The final chapter discusses the question of change. To what extent do members of Parliament accept that reform is required or would be helpful and to what extent is there consensus on the kind of changes which might be fruitful? Could the reality of the job fit the expectations of the original aspirants more satisfactorily than at

present? And will anything ever be changed, despite the acknowledged strain imposed by the long and late hours, the growing
constituency demands, and the ever-increasing weight of the
legislative programme, while MPs themselves are uncertain about
ends and divided on priorities?

1

The Role of the Honourable Member

*People do not demand resounding
oratory, or constant attendance in
the chamber ... nor do voters
require ... an assiduous scrutineer
or amender of legislation....
They want a county councillor at
Westminster.*

(The Granada survey)

In the days immediately following a general election, the Palace of
Westminster seems full of earnest young men, in dark suits and
striped shirts, walking purposefully about the place. Only on close
inspection does their determined composure and self-confident
manner occasionally slip to reveal an underlying uncertainty. They
mostly look as if they are striding from committee room to office; in
fact, many of them have little knowledge of the House's committee
procedure and, perhaps even more disconcertingly, most of them
have no office. They are the new men (and men they overwhelmingly are; some 90 per cent of the House of Commons has always
been male) of the new parliament, and for many the job to which
they have just been elected is a bit of a mystery.

Despite strong political views and a commitment to the party
which has put them in the House, most have only the haziest
notion as to the job they are expected to do. As one succinctly put
it, 'You spend so much time and energy getting into the place, you
just don't have time to think about what you're supposed to do
when you get there.' Even if the time were available however, and
aspiring MPs were always of the contemplative and assiduous
variety, they would probably still find it difficult immediately to
identify the essential features of their new role.

Nor is the problem theirs alone. A considerable amount of

academic effort has, over time, gone into the analysis of the parliamentary role, the procedures of the House and the process of legislation. Much less common, however, are accounts of what MPs actually do, of what the job amounts to. One may search in vain the pages of the great classic works of parliamentary procedure or constitutional law for more than a passing reference to the role of the honourable member. Dicey, for example, deals at length with the powers and privileges of Parliament as a collective entity but largely ignores its individual membership.[1] Erskine May traces the history of procedure and the development of party politics but says almost nothing about the backbencher.[2] Similarly, Wade and Phillips' *Constitutional Law* mentions members only in passing, mainly in relation to privilege, and gives no account, for example, of the qualifications for, or requirements of, the job.[3]

A JOB DESCRIPTION?

Is the job, then, so amorphous, even ephemeral, that it defies all attempts at identification? Most jobs require some training or experience, have some specifiable duties and at least a limited right of tenure. Does the representative's job have any equivalent parameters? The short answer is probably 'no'. There is no formal training for politics, no Institute of Political Success issuing diplomas in electoral behaviour or certificates in local activist management – and a university degree in political science is no particular advantage in the quest for a safe seat. There are no neatly printed job descriptions, no terms of service, no contract. The duties are inexact and, above all, there is no security of tenure. And, yet, it may be possible to give an account of the job, and of the perceptions of those who do it, without ending up with either an 'ideal type' which refers to no job done by any actual person, or simply a specific description of 'one man's week'. Slightly to adapt Wittgenstein, 'the job is not a something, but not a nothing either'; it has certain common identifiable aspects and it is these which will be developed and examined in the course of this book.

The job we shall explore here is the job of the backbencher, not of ministers or their shadows in the opposition. The ministerial role is a distinct and different one, almost exclusively focused on a particular department of state and often with the considerable back-up and resources which the department can offer. The minister's job too, is fairly clearly delineated, and demands the development of specialist knowledge. By contrast, the back-bencher is a jack-of-all-trades, carving out his or her own role within the constraints imposed by parliamentary procedures, the available facilities of the House and the ever-present demands of constituents. The qualifications for the job, as we shall see in Chapter 2, mostly turn out, on inspection, to be disqualifications of people in certain categories from even standing for election in the first place. But there is, for example, no special age qualification – beyond the requirement that the candidate must be twenty–one – such as is demanded of American politicians, where representatives must be at least twenty-five years old, senators thirty years old, and the President a minimum of thirty-five. Again, no residency qualification is demanded. Whereas in other countries, the aspiring politician is expected to show his or her representativeness by living in the constituency, no such requirement is made of British MPs. And no particular educational or technical attainments are needed.

DELEGATE OR REPRESENTATIVE?

Whereas the limited formal requirements for the job have remained fairly constant over time, the job itself has changed considerably in scope and content. People's expectations and MPs' own perceptions have also been modified, and it is perhaps not surprising that, as we shall see, members themselves differ in their views of the main features of the job. The extent, for example, of members' independence of judgement has been hotly contested since at least the eighteenth century. In earlier times, however, the strongest ties between a member and his constituents were assumed and his duty was seen as fulfilled in being their agent. In the days when Parliament (or at least the Commons) existed largely to grant taxes to the monarch and occasionally to present petitions for the redress of grievances, the primary loyalty of members was to those whom they represented. Members were seen as local representatives, living in their constituencies and often being maintained by them. It is recorded that, in 1339, the Commons were asked to grant monies to the king and collectively replied that they could not do so without consulting the commons of the country and therefore suggested that another parliament be summoned, specifically mandated, as it were, on this issue.[4]

The payment of members by their constituents tied them effectively to the interests of their paymasters. For example, the poet, Andrew Marvell, was member for Hull from 1660 to 1678. There was, of course, no universal suffrage at the time and he was chosen simply by the mayor and aldermen of the town, with whom he corresponded frequently on political issues and proceedings in Parliament. There was no question for Marvell about where his responsibility lay. Indeed, he directly asks for and receives directions on how he should perform in the House: 'I desire that you will . . . consider whether there be anything that particularly relates to the state of your town, or of your neighbouring country . . . whereof you may think fit to advertise me, and therein to give me your instructions, to which I shall carefully conform.' A hundred years later, however, any such careful conformity was being rendered distinctly suspect by Edmund Burke, who, well before the Great Reform Act of 1832, was claiming a wider national duty for honourable members. When, in 1774, he was first elected for the Bristol constituency, he told his supporters exactly where his priorities lay:

> Certainly, Gentlemen, it ought to be the happiness and glory of a representative to live in the strictest union, the closest correspondence, and the most unreserved communication with his constituents. Their wishes ought to have great weight with him; their opinions high respect; their business unremitted attention. It is his duty to sacrifice his repose, his pleasures, his satisfaction to theirs, – and above all, ever, and in all cases, to prefer their interest to his own.

But, he continues, 'his unbiased opinion, his mature judgment, his enlightened conscience, he ought not to sacrifice to you, to any man or any set of men living. . . Your representative owes you not his industry only, but his judgment; and he betrays, instead of serving you, if he sacrifices it to your opinion.'[5]

Burke's classic statement here, and his further belief that 'Parliament is not a congress of ambassadors from different and hostile interests . . . but a deliberative assembly of one nation, with one interest, that of the whole . . .'[6] has formed the basis of the argument ever since of those who hold that the MP, although the representative of his constituents, is certainly not simply their agent, sent to Westminster merely as a mouthpiece. This has probably been the commonly held view of the Conservative and Liberal MPs ever since. However, the Labour Party's position here has been rather more complicated, with some of its MPs believing that they were indeed the delegates of their constituency parties, which would have the right to deselect them if they did not satisfactorily reflect constituency activist opinion.

Part of the reason for the difference of view about this fundamental role of the MP is to be found in the historical development of the parties themselves. With the movement to universal suffrage in the nineteenth and early twentieth centuries, the existing parties took steps to consolidate their support in the country with the new electorate. Peel was the first to realise that the voters were now a potent extra-parliamentary force in politics, and with his Tamworth Manifesto appealed to his constituents, in 1834, on the basis of party policy. Thus grew up a local party structure designed to serve the parliamentary party, raise funds and get out the vote at elections. The Labour Party, on the other hand, was formed after the establishment of manhood suffrage, specifically to represent the working class, and Labour MPs were always expected to be the servants of the people. The idea of the representative as agent and the consequent need for extra-parliamentary supervision of the Parliamentary Labour Party is therefore not new: as Miliband says, from the beginning, 'Underlying the tension between activists and parliamentarians was the former's fear that the Labour group in Parliament would, if it were not strictly controlled, backslide into opportunism, manoeuvre and compromise.'[7] All these tensions came to a head in the late 1970s when many party activists blamed the failure of successive Labour governments to introduce sufficiently socialist measures on the treachery of the parliamentary leadership. The claim that only mandatory reselection of MPs could bridge the gap between members and their supporters in the constituencies gathered support, and this is now official Labour Party policy.

THE MEMBER AND THE CONSTITUENCY

The question of whether the member owes his primary loyalty to

his constituents or to his conscience has also been complicated by
the growth of party power. Burke's claim to individual autonomy
for the member is perhaps rather less compelling when put in the
modern context of tight party discipline, where MPs owe their
seats largely to their adoption by the particular party. If the
electorate votes mainly for parties rather than for individuals, it is
hard not to agree with Roy Hattersley that the 'promise of
unfettered judgement ... [is] the product of a less educated and
more deferential age. In the era of party manifestoes and party
whips, it is a romantic fiction.'[8] However, the debate about the
nature of the MP's role here continues and, as we shall see, MPs of
all parties sometimes claim to be independent of their parties, at
least to the extent of being prepared, if they judge it necessary, to
refuse to accept the party line.

Independence from the party is one thing; independence from
constituencies is another, and most MPs are increasingly aware of
the importance of their constituency role if they hope for a long
and secure tenure of the job. The importance of local issues, and
specifically of constituents' problems, has made the member's job
more akin, in many cases, to that of a social worker than to that of a
legislator. Thus there develops a tension, which many members
find difficult to resolve, between the job in the House of Commons
and the job in the home base – the constituency. The member
depends on the support of the constituency for selection and
continuance in post, as much in the other parties as in the Labour
Party. Conservative MPs who have failed to keep the loyalty of
their constituency parties have paid the price by losing their seats.
Humphrey Berkeley in Lancaster, Nigel Nicolson in Bournemouth
East and Christchurch, and Reader Harris in Heston and Isleworth
are all examples of Conservative members who lost their seats
after a disagreement with their local party. Most local party
supporters want an MP they feel they can trust to represent their
interests and not a 'national figure' or a potential prime minister,
who is much too liable to be spending time cultivating his or her
own future career than tending to the needs of local people.
As Ivor Crewe has found, for most people, 'the ideal MP is a
local resident who devotes his full time to the job of dealing
with their personal problems and ... occasionally sallies forth to
express his constituents' views in the national debate at
Westminster'.[9]

If this were the end of the story, the answer for the ambitious member, keen to hang on to the job, would seem clear; 'pavement politics' is the name of the game and the priority is the making and maintaining of a high profile locally, based on good works. The victories of David Alton in Liverpool and Simon Hughes in Bermondsey are examples of long devotion to the battle against damp housing and inadequate street lighting finally paying off. Yet many MPs want to play in another arena, that of the national debate in the House of Commons, and may find themselves there pursuing a role that, if not diametrically opposed to the constituency role, is at least very different from it. The fact is that they may resent what they see as the 'trivialisation' of their role into that of constituency errand boy. As one said, to say that someone is 'A Very Good Constituency Member', a term of approbation with the local party, is to say that 'you don't count in the House of Commons'.[10] Yet, in order to have the opportunity to pursue a national career; as a policy specialist or ultimately a Cabinet minister, a constituency is a *sine qua non*. Without it, there is no national career' it is the base of the greasy pole which the ambitious aspire to climb to national fame and fortune.

Aware of this, few disdain their local party, and most who do live to regret it. Dick Taverne believed in retrospect that he might have survived his upsets at Lincoln if he had spent more time 'drinking with the lads'.[11] He did not cultivate the locals and, in the end, they ceased to cultivate him. Indeed, the more an MP takes an independent line at Westminster, the more he may need his local base, which must be served both by rallying the troops against the political enemy and by pursuing local interests and solving local problems. Local supporters are much less interested in the rights and wrongs of party policy than in having their convictions strengthened and their beliefs upheld. 'If the wisdom of party policy is questioned publicly in a way that suggests some slight merit for the views of opponents, party enthusiasts are scandalised.'[12] Most MPs are probably aware of this to the extent of maintaining a strictly simplistic style of oratory in addressing their activists. Julian Critchley refers, with some admiration, to the speech notes of a Conservative colleague called on to inspire the faithful. These amounted to just three points, on which he was able to expostulate for half an hour or more: 'a) twenty years of ceaseless fight against Socialism b) flogging and hanging c) Mrs. Thatcher'.[13] Even if his account is characteristically somewhat tongue-in-cheek, it makes its point.

THE MP AS SOCIAL WORKER OR SPECIALIST?

If rallying the party faithful is an important part of the local job, so too is the very public provision of an efficient welfare service for constituents. Not only does this allow the MP to work closely with the activists, but it also gets him known as a local figure. Those who denigrate the importance of such work are probably only on firm ground if their constituencies are very low in social deprivation; for most, the position is more accurately reflected by Ken Weetch MP, who had for a time the only Labour seat in East Anglia: 'I catch the slates as they fall off the roofs.'

The increase in the importance of constituency work is only one of the changes in the job over the past years; another has been brought about by the great increase in the amount and complexity of legislation. As the Kilbrandon Report pointed out, of the 718 parliamentary questions answered in June 1971, between 80 and 90 per cent would not have been answered in 1900 because they would not have been the concern of government.[14] The volume of legislation, too, has much increased. In 1900, Public Acts amounted to about 200 pages, as compared with nearly 2000 in 1974.[15] The results of this increased scope and detail of Parliament's job is reflected in the reduction of private members' time, the greater use of standing Committees, and the lengthening of the parliamentary session from an average of 129 days before 1914 to 163 since 1945.[16]

The outcome of all this for MPs is the increasing pressure to acquire some expertise; to develop a specialism or two, amongst the vast and disconcerting array of modern political concerns, on which they can contribute with some authority. Whether MPs ought to be 'experts' or 'generalists' is a question which has been raised by numbers of academic commentators, at least since the Fulton Report on the Civil Service suggested that our administrators should no longer be drawn mainly from the ranks of the literati, educated in Greek but ignorant of econometrics.[17] The view was extended to include Parliament and parliamentarians when the argument was made, by Richard Crossman and others, that a non-specialist House of Commons could not perform its function of check on the executive if the work of the executive was becoming too complex for the House even to understand. Part of the answer to this was thought to lie in the development of the Select Committee system, which, it was hoped, would allow a specialist committee of the House to develop an expertise in a particular subject area and to call as witnesses ministers and civil servants to explain their policies. The theory was that this information would then be transmitted back to the House, which could proceed with its task on an informed basis. How these committees have operated in practice will be dealt with in Chapter 3, while MPs' views of their effectiveness will be covered in Chapter 7. For the moment, two points can be made about the effects of a wider political involvement on the MP's role. First, the development of Select Committees has not meant the establishment, as some foretold it would, of a new career path in Parliament, a new route to the top. Experts may be admired for their specialist contribution, but this is still not normally the way to make a political name. Select Committees have not, for example, become the equivalent in this respect of Congressional Committees in the American system. There, the chairmen of the most prestigious of these groups, in the House and Senate, have a political standing second to none. They outlive presidents and many ambitious representatives see membership of such centres of power as the ultimate political achievement. Not so in the House of Commons, where few would see them in this light and most would probably agree with Archy Kirkwood's assessment that they can 'often seem to be experts talking to other experts and the specialist press'.

Still, some individuals have undoubtedly benefited from the ability to use their expertise in the more specialised environment of a Select Committee and have become more widely known and respected in the process. Terence Higgins, for example, was not a favourite of the Conservative administration from 1979 onwards; although a senior backbench Tory, his views on social affairs were considered rather too liberal and his economic analysis too 'intellectual' for the government's taste. Before the advent of Select Committees he might well have found himself and his considerable talent lost on the backbenches. However, as chairman of the Treasury and Civil Service Select Committee, he commands both greater status and an enviable *entrée* into economic debates. Similarly, Sir Anthony Kershaw, and David Howell who followed him as chairman of the Foreign Affairs Committee, had a platform for their views, both inside and outside the House, which they could never have commanded as ordinary backbenchers, however well-informed.

The second point which emerges from the realisation that

Parliament now performs a much wider role in society than in the past, with legislation covering almost every aspect of life, is that this diffusion of interest has also meant a loss of concentrated power. As Ghita Ionescu points out, Parliament now shares power with many other institutions, such as the trade unions, CBI, numerous pressure groups, the EEC and so on, all of which demand a share in the policy-making process.[18] And, although Parliament retains sovereignty, this has made the political world, as he says, a 'shrinking' one; 'being *at* the centre [of political decision-making] is not ... the same as *being* the centre'.[19]

This is not to say, as is sometimes suggested, that this 'shrinking world' of politics is necessarily an inferior one. People often seem to hark back to some sort of golden age when discussing the status and significance of Parliament and parliamentarians. This nostalgia for the 'great days' of the House was summed up by *The Times* in 1957 in the complaint that Parliament contained 'far too many little men' and concerned itself with irrelevant 'fighting over things that do not matter'.[20] Yet, 'twas ever thus. As Laski reminds us, Gladstone in the 1880s was lamenting the decline in the status and quality of the backbencher as compared with his equivalent earlier in the nineteenth century.[21] Although it is true that the backgrounds of members have changed recently, and the job of a representative has lost status with the erosion of the unquestioned prestige of all professionals (see Chapter 2), the grumble about 'little men' may not be fair. Even so, as we shall see, the public has an increasingly low opinion of MPs and their general contribution.

PUBLIC PERCEPTIONS OF THE MEMBER OF PARLIAMENT

One important reason why Parliament now comes in for greater criticism than ever before is the public perception of Westminster through the broadcasting media. Opposing the idea that the House in the 1950s was more badly behaved than that of earlier times, Lord Winterton, himself an MP of long standing, claimed from personal experience that they were 'like a Sunday school in comparison with the 1906 and two 1910 Parliaments'.[22] Broadcasting has made people aware of the idiosyncratic mores of the Chamber, with its booing and hear-hearing so reminiscent of a school debating society. All that has changed is that the general public is now more conscious of this day by day.

Much of what has been said depends on the ideas of academic commentators about the job of the MP. It is perhaps worth establishing, however, what the public, those who choose the honourable members, actually think of them and of their role. The glib answer has to be – not much. Butler and Stokes found that 'The MP does not loom very large in the electors' consciousness' and that less than half of their respondents could even name their own member of Parliament.[23] More than this, they found that, in general, the electorate do not believe that their MPs have done anything for their constituencies (only one in seven could think of something here).[24] Again, opinion polls reveal a rather jaundiced view of the representative. An NOP survey in 1968 showed that the great majority of people (78 per cent) thought that 'most politicians will promise anything to get votes', and only 18 per cent of the sample disagreed. The same poll found that 66 per cent believed that 'most politicians care more about party than the country', and that 60 per cent were convinced that politicians told the truth only when it suited them.[25] Overall, as Christopher Mayhew says, the main criticisms against MPs seem to be that 'they have too little influence, that they are too subservient to their party whips, that they are too often "out for themselves", and that the methods they use are sometimes too devious'.[26]

There have been very few full-scale surveys of the public's attitude to politicians. Almost the only recent work was that done for Granada Television in 1972, which found that most people believed that politics and government were simply too complicated to understand.[27] The general impression gained from the Granada survey is of an overwhelming ignorance of Parliament, its demands and procedures, and a consequent lack of reality in the expectations about what MPs can do. The clearest result of the survey, however, is that most people were only interested in the local involvement of their member. When asked to choose amongst a list of duties which members might be expected to carry out, the three most often quoted were: expressing voters' concerns about national issues, dealing with constituents' personal problems, and attending meetings in the constituency. As the survey concludes, 'People do not demand resounding oratory or constant attendance in the chamber . . . nor do voters require . . . an assiduous scrutineer and amender of legislation. . . . They want a county councillor at

Westminster.' This is a finding confirmed over and over again in surveys and opinion polls. The only cases in which people seem willing to concede a certain distance between the member and the constituency is where the sitting MP becomes a 'star' – but only a well-known cabinet minister or prime minister will normally qualify. Here, pride in the celebrity of the local representative may compensate for the loss in local orientation. In addition, well-known senior ministers almost always have safe seats, which in the Tory case would normally be in an area of low social deprivation, where the constituency role would be considerably less, and in the Labour case would usually mean a well-organised and supportive local party, equipped to deal by itself with most local problems.

The Granada survey also confirmed the public's lack of awareness of their members' interests and connections. Less than a quarter (23 per cent) could say anything at all about their MP's record in Parliament and most were consequently almost completely unaware of the member's business or professional interests, union connections, involvements with lobbies, and so forth. The cynicism found in past surveys about the motives and integrity of politicians was also reflected in the survey, 40 per cent agreeing that 'most politicians were in it for what they could get out of it'.

MPs have nearly always fared badly when ranked by the public against other professions. In an ORC survey of 1974, a mere 4 per cent of those asked picked out MPs as one of the two most trustworthy professions (only businessmen and merchant bankers did worse). In a later poll, conducted for the *Daily Mail* in May 1982, only 3 per cent 'most admired' politicians out of a list of twelve professions (this time only company directors did worse). In similar vein, the television consumer programme *Watchdog* reported the results of a 1985 Mori poll on public esteem for various occupations. Again, MPs were ranked third from the bottom (coming before journalists and door-to-door salesmen) in degree of trustworthiness.[28] This said, the public do seem to display a considerable degree of schizophrenia when it comes to assessing their own representative, especially if they have sought help or received assistance. As the Granada survey shows, 'whereas "politicians" are incompetent and dishonourable, "my MP" is well-intentioned and tries hard'.

Of wider interest is a Mori poll carried out in 1985 for the

Economist, which showed a House of Commons 'declining in public esteem' and 'doing a poor job in controlling the work of government'.[29] The *Economist* claimed that the public view of the Commons and MPs had degenerated significantly since a similar poll in 1973, which had indicated greater public interest in politics. More than half the 1985 sample thought the main functions of an MP were to 'express voter concern about issues' and 'deal with constituents' personal problems'. Even more constituency-biased were the 28 per cent who said the MP's *most important* role was to 'attend meetings in his constituency'. These findings are particularly interesting when compared with the results of the Commons All-Party Reform Group survey (see Chapter 7), where MPs were themselves asked to rank such roles and only 27 per cent of them thought that acting as a local ombudsman was very important. On the other hand, 45 per cent of MPs rated 'acting as a check on the executive' highly, whereas the public rate this very low. Clearly, and probably unsurprisingly, although MPs are aware of public opinion, they do not express the same priorities or hold the same views about the balance of the job as do their constituents.

MPs' PERCEPTIONS OF THEIR JOB

Just how MPs do see the job will emerge in the course of this study as we consider their views of their parliamentary role and how it might be changed; their notions of constituency work; their involvements with their party and their interests outside the House; their expectations of the job before they came into Parliament and their informed view of the reality once they are there. Most of them believe that they work very hard. Many years ago, Lord Snell claimed that 'the average MP works at greater pressure and for longer hours than nine-tenths of those who elect him . . . if the average factory worker, miner or engineer had the same strain put upon him, he would down tools within a month and demand better conditions of work'.[30] In much the same vein, but in vastly greater detail, T. B. Langton, then a backbench MP, wrote to *The Times* in 1957 cataloguing the demands on a member's time:

he is expected to be abreast of all current problems – local, national and international. He is expected to know the contents of every national, local, daily and weekly newspaper, to know the answers to the hundreds of questions fired at him; to answer his voluminous mail promptly . . . to subscribe liberally to local charities, clubs and societies . . . to visit the numerous branches of his constituency and make well-prepared and authoritative speeches; to make regular speeches in the House of Commons; to spend long hours, Monday to Friday, in the House of Commons . . . to keep up his voting record; to spend long hours on Saturdays dancing like a performing bear from fête to fête; . . . to desert his wife and family, and to a large extent the business or job by which he supports them, in order to serve his constituents.

And in case the point is not yet made, he continues that the MP is expected to do all this 'for scarcely enough remuneration to pay for his secretary, mail, travelling expenses, living expenses in London, subscriptions and donations, reading matter etc., let alone compensate him for the loss of his home life and business time'.[31]

By 1963, MPs didn't think the job was much better. An *Observer* survey showed them discontented with their pay and conditions (77 per cent); unsure of their influence (44 per cent); unconvinced of their own efficiency (only 15 per cent believed the House did its work competently).[32] The same kind of views still prevail: salaries are constantly pronounced too low; conditions in the Palace of Westminster itself are Dickensian, prompting one MP to describe it as 'an elegant gothic slum'.[33] Above all, MPs are uncertain about the balance of their own role; just how far they are supposed to be super-social workers, or first and foremost good House of Commons members, is, for many of them, not clear, and the uncertainty adds to the strain of the job. Not all MPs, of course, allow this serious state of affairs to depress them: James Wellbeloved once commented that, in spite of its frustrations, being in Parliament is better than working, and, more seriously, but with equal irreverence, Austin Mitchell MP has said that the job could only be done successfully by 'a peculiarly thick-skinned egomaniac workaholic who had a populist's rapport with people but an intellectual's understanding of problems and issues'.[34]

The growth in constituency involvement by MPs is not, of course, simply a passive reaction to greater local demands; members contribute to it by their own activities, by being available, by publicising their surgeries and their services, by answering letters promptly. And, although not all are forced to be immersed in local problems – as Julian Critchley says, 'a lot depends on the kind of constituency . . . if you have a safe seat in an area of nil unemployment . . . you're left with only a relatively small amount of constituency surgery work to do' – most choose to spend a lot of their time in that way. They make themselves available and sometimes seem 'embarrassingly eager for customers'; for, as Austin Mitchell goes on, however much they grumble at the growing load, 'in fact, they love it. It gives them a sense of usefulness, a sense of purpose. . . .'[35]

Being given 'a sense of purpose' makes MPs sound suspiciously like the casualties of some social disaster, in need of direction and personal security. The idea of constituency politics as therapy, however, is perhaps not so odd as it might initially appear. Most MPs play, and are well aware that they play, very little part in the policy-making process. (In a later chapter we discuss the general belief that 'policy is made by a few ministers'.) Governments increasingly see their role as putting their programme, for which they claim an electoral mandate, into practice. As John Mackintosh put it, 'in both parties, the MP feels powerless in the face of the Cabinet and the civil service when the party is in government and in the face of the party bureaucracy when in opposition'.[36]

In the light of this, constituency work is a welcome assertion of autonomy and influence. There, the MP is free to pursue the problems he or she chooses to consider important; the party line as such is not at issue and, almost regardless of the outcome, the member has won local support. Constituency work is undertaken at a sometimes frantic rate, not just because it secures the future by creating local goodwill and a high profile, but also because members find it fulfilling. Time and again members say in interview (and the results of surveys confirm this) that they find constituency work the 'most satisfying' or 'most rewarding' part of the job. Here they know what is expected of them – though many point out that this role is often not much more than to provide a sympathetic ear – and they are rewarded accordingly. It is perhaps an index of the ambiguity of the job that some members express a kind of bemused surprise and others a touching gratitude at the responses they have had from constituents with whose cases they had dealt. Roger Freeman MP, who has wide experience of business and banking, makes this point when he says, 'I'm amazed by the nice letters people write even when you've scarcely been able to do anything. It's not at all like business, where nobody thanks you unless you deliver.'

And yet, for all its attractions for MPs who habitually feel unloved and undervalued, constituency work is, as some describe it, 'parish pump'. Indeed, one might think that it is to escape exactly this sort of involvement that many politicians move on from being local councillors to become honourable members. Although it consistently figures as the best part of the job on members' own evaluation, constituency work is, in the words of Bob Litherland MP and a former councillor, irreducibly concerned with 'the endless pursuit of ephemera and minutiae', and thus 'very pedestrian. . . . Quite honestly, sometimes I ask myself what have I done today? What world-shattering effect have I had? and it's very little. . . .'[37]

This, of course, is part of a general complaint about the value and prestige of the MP's role. Members seem often to be asking themselves if they really are important and valued people. In their constituencies, it is easier to convince themselves that they are; at Westminster, however, it is another story. As one 1979 new boy, Alexander Pollock, put it, 'You have to be schizophrenic; in the constituency you are treated like a VIP: wherever you go people want to meet you, want to hear what you think. At Westminster, you just become an unknown again and nobody's particularly interested in your contribution.' It must come as a sad blow to many of those who have struggled so hard to get into the Commons to feel, when the triumph has worn off, that the game was scarcely worth the candle.

STRESSES AND STRAINS OF THE JOB

Perhaps all this is simply one of a set of irreconcilable and contradictory demands which make the job so stressful. It has much in common with that of clergymen, who also deal daily with a world set by other people's demands. Responding to this requires a flexibility which makes it hard to develop a regular timetable or a clear job description. For some, this is part of the charm of the job: in it you can create your own priorities and largely work your own hours. Yet it also encourages a rather unstructured existence with which, not surprisingly, many find it difficult to deal.[38] Clergymen, like MPs, are also expected to be omniscient, to have a view on everything and to be self-confident and articulate. Many know they fail to live up to this image and the stress of attempting it may be considerable. Both professions also abound with examples of what Karen Horney calls the 'helping personality', which sees itself as 'being essentially loving and . . . motivated by the wish to be a helpful, considerate, concerned, compassionate and affectionate person'.[39]

However, as several writers have pointed out, it is uncertain whether the helping personality's primary need is to love or to be loved. Being concerned and involved with others is one way of gaining love, admiration and approval. Yet, in both jobs there is also a 'leadership' dimension which requires, rather than the capacity to be sympathetic and concerned, the ability to take a stand, to make decisions, and, if necessary, to be unpopular. Such conflicts, in the case of clergymen, have led one writer to talk of the 'inner stress' generated by this 'success-love polarity' and to suggest that, in some cases, it may be the cause of aggressive or rebellious behaviour.[40] At least one MP claims to have seen the same tendency in the Commons: 'like moths around a flame', says Leo Abse, 'the aggressive flutter around Westminster. Outside Dartmoor and the armed forces, there are no more aggressive men than those sitting in our Parliament.'[41] A more likely analysis may simply be that such cross-pressured individuals will retreat into constituency work, which they perhaps inevitably see as the most rewarding part of the job, bringing a large helping of much-needed ego-boosting and virtually no conflict.

Undoubtedly one of the most exhausting aspects of the job is its exposed nature. MPs are the possessions of their public and the importance of appearances is great. Sexual and alcoholic binges are not necessarily the kiss of death, but indiscretion often is. Cecil Parkinson's long affair with his secretary did not impede his successful rise within his party, but his failure to control its much-publicised ending was enough to lose him, if only temporarily, his seat in the Cabinet. Probably greater these days, however, than the stigma of marital upset (after all, the divorce rate in the United Kingdom as a whole is now around one in three) is that of illness. Lord Moran, his doctor, chronicles the lengths to which family and colleagues went to keep Churchill's illness from the public, both during and after the war.[42] Any suggestion of mental stress is particularly damaging; politicians are expected to cope, not just with their own problems but also with those of the rest of us, and the spectacle of their failing to do so is apparently profoundly distressing to a public that longs to put its faith in the all-knowing, all-doing MP. In the American context, Senator Eagleton felt it necessary to resign as vice-presidential candidate when it became known that he had seen a psychiatrist, and this in a country where being 'in analysis' is a not uncommon pastime of the middle classes. In Britain, there was much press speculation when, after the 1983 election, David Steel took a short sabbatical. Other professionals may be encouraged occasionally to take stock, *reculer pour mieux sauter*, but not, apparently, politicians, for whom being seen to be constantly in command is part of the job.

WHY DO THEY DO IT?

With all those pressures to face, the uncertainty of the job and the insecurity of tenure, one may be forgiven for asking why anybody would want to become a backbencher. When the question is put, some MPs become flippant. Rupert Allason, for example, said (with some irony: he is a successful writer) that he came in because he couldn't get a 'proper job'. But for many, their interest in politics started very early. The importance of family connections is well established at Westminster (indeed, Allason himself is the son of an MP). In 1987, for example, 30 of the MPs elected were themselves the sons or daughters of ex-MPs. One, Andrew Mitchell, was the son of a sitting MP, David Mitchell; two husband and wife teams were returned (the Wintertons and the Bottomleys); and Hilary Armstrong succeeded her father in Durham North-West.[43] Family background, even without such direct Westminster involvement, is often crucial in motivating a young political hopeful. Paul Boateng had a father who was a Cabinet minister in Ghana and a politically active mother. Graham Allen's miner father had passionate political views and 'talked a lot'. Such early influences clearly shape political ideas and emphasise the importance of political action.

The desire to change things is a strong motivating factor with many members. They see what they believe to be maladministration, inefficient organisation or a need for reform and believe that it is at Westminster that the required changes can be effected. Some have a specific interest which they want to promote, like Ronnie Fearn, whose involvement with youth work and education went back 20 years. Others have a general belief in the need for social change, like Hugo Summerson who, disgruntled with the state of the country, believed that the best way to do something about it was to become an MP. For some members, there is obviously great pleasure in the job. They do it because it is exactly what they want to do. Gillian Shephard, for example, says she 'positively loves it', the variety, the people, the constituency and the House. 'We eat cake in this job, not bread', she says, reflecting the joy in politics which those outside often find difficult to understand. But it is this intoxicating feeling of being at the centre of things, of making things happen, of contributing to decisions that matter, which constitutes for most MPs a main reason for doing the job.

Few of the backbenchers we interviewed were willing to admit to the pursuit of power as a motive for political involvement, though James Arbuthnot is clear that he aims at a Cabinet job, and Gillian Shephard maintains 'Anyone in politics wants to be where policy is made.' Andrew Mitchell says firmly 'I don't think there is anything wrong with ambition' – explaining, 'People who go into politics do so from a mixture of altruism, and egotism. If they are totally egotistical then their constituents might as well go hang. If they are totally altruistic they should be social workers.' Most MPs agreed that they wanted to change things; that they liked being in a position to help people, but they denied seeking power for its own sake. Perhaps this is simply being honest. Backbenchers, as more than one member pointed out, have influence, but very little individual power. Perhaps too, it reflects the desire of so many MPs, recognising this, to move on from the backbenches as quickly as possible. As is sometimes said, the Commons is increasingly full of hungry young men who want the Cabinet quickly rather than a knighthood slowly. And this, in its turn, may be indicative of the greater 'professionalisation' of politics.

ARE MPs PROFESSIONALS?

Although it may have its similarities with the clergyman's job, politics has little in common with the other professions. Indeed, it may be questioned whether politicians are 'professionals' in any significant sense at all. In most of the studies of professions and professionals, the term assumes a 'professed knowledge of some department of learning or science' and it is perhaps therefore unsurprising that, in their work on the subject, Lewis and Maude discuss the claims to professionalism of, *inter alia*, actors, actuaries, advertisers, airline pilots, barbers, brokers, chiropodists, dentists, economists, estate agents, musicians, surveyors and veterinary surgeons but never mention politicians.[44] However, it has become increasingly popular to talk, if not of professional, then of *career*, politicians. In the past MPs were often part-time, maintaining their main career interests elsewhere than in Parliament; or they came into Parliament later in life, having made a career and some necessary money elsewhere, before embarking on their political life. But, as Walkland points out, for an 'increasing number of post-war MPs . . . a parliamentary career . . . is no longer an adjunct to nor an interruption of their careers outside the House'.[45] Colin Mellors, in his study of British MPs, suggests that career status is won when a member has served for ten years or more at Westminster and, on this criterion, about two-thirds of MPs become 'professionals'.[46]

In charting the rise of the career politician in British politics, Anthony King concentrates less on objective criteria such as length of service and emphasises rather the commitment of such an individual. 'He regards politics as his vocation, he seeks fulfilment in politics, he sees his future in politics, he would be deeply upset if circumstances forced him to retire from politics. In short, he is hooked.'[47] King goes on to quote Lord Kilmuir, who, as David Maxwell-Fyfe, had a long career in the Commons, and who admitted that, from the first, 'the world of politics entranced me. It is like some kind of virus infection; it is very difficult to convey to the unafflicted the symptoms or the nature of the disease.'[48]

That there has been a change in the kind of people entering politics, their backgrounds and experience, is incontestable, as Chapter 2 shows; what is less certain is the extent to which such a change in personnel has changed the job itself. It seems likely that politicians have become more experienced politically; but at the same time more and more of them have little knowledge of the world outside politics. As they become more ambitious, more partisan, so too they may become more entrenched and more dogmatic. To have full-time, hard-working *career* politicians, in other words, is not costless. The public may believe it gets a better deal from such tireless and committed individuals, training themselves all their lives for their political goals; they might also remember Shaw's sardonic suggestion that those who single-mindedly pursue public office should be considered to have disqualified themselves from holding it!

The 'job' which has been outlined so far is undoubtedly rather vague. It has changed over time and it differs in scope and balance from member to member. It is difficult therefore to set parameters, and one sympathises with the children in Olive Stevens' study who, when asked what MPs did, found the indisputable lowest common factor: 'they talk'.[49] Indeed they do; but they also have other characteristics and preoccupations in common. The job is more of a menu than a set meal: within the constraints of the dishes offered, MPs will choose, guided by their own perceptions of their constituency, their majority, their party's strength in the House and so on, what their priorities are. Searing identifies four different roles which backbenchers typically take up and leave at different points in their careers. These are ministerial aspirant; parliament man; policy advocate; and constituency member.[50] Not all MPs, of course, pursue all of them, but most will veer to one of them at any particular time and their views are revealed in the roles they deem to be most important. Whether they think they should be full-orpart-time is another factor which will probably affect their notions of appropriate pay, conditions and facilities. The idea of a new breed of 'career' politician, too, will have to be explored in the context not only of how members come into the House, but of what their business, professional and other involvements are outside. Is constituency work increasing for all MPs, and, if so, do even 'constituency members' involve themselves here simply to gain favour with their local supporters, from higher motives of public service, or because they also find it comforting and rewarding in a job which has more than its share of back-biting and insecurity. Has the increase in professionalism created a House of Commons full of ambitious young men and women who all want to be ministers? Is the backbencher's job now only a phase in the rise and rise of the career politician?

These are some of the questions which need to be raised in identifying the present-day job of an MP, and in saying what the job might be. The rest of this book is, with the help of the MPs themselves, our attempt to suggest at least some of the answers.

NOTES

1. A. V. Dicey, *The Law of the Constitution* (Macmillan, 1908).
2. Sir Thomas Erskine May, *The Constitutional History of England* (Longmans Green, 1912). See also his *Parliamentary Practice*, 20th edn, ed. Sir C. Gordon (Butterworth, 1983).
3. E. C. S. Wade and G. G. Phillips, *Constitutional Law*, 5th edn (Longmans Green, 1957) pp. 119–25.
4. Quoted in C. Ilbert, *Parliament, its History, Constitution, and Practice* (Home University Library, 1929) pp. 160–1.
5. E. Burke, 'Speech to the Electors of Bristol', in Burke, *On Government, Politics and Society*, ed. B. W. Hill (Fontana, 1975) p. 157.
6. Ibid., p. 158.
7. R. Miliband, *Parliamentary Socialism: A Study in the Politics of Labour* (Allen and Unwin, 1961) p. 26.
8. *The Times*, 14 July 1981.
9. I. Crewe and J. Spence, 'Parliament and Public', *New Society*, July 1973.
10. Quoted by D. Searing in 'The Role of the Good Constituency Member and the Practice of Representation in Great Britain', *Journal of Politics*, 47 (1985) 364.
11. See D. Taverne, *The Future of the Left* (Cape, 1974).
12. P. G. Richards, *The Backbenchers* (Faber and Faber, 1972) p. 162.
13. J. Critchley, *Westminster Blues: Minor Chords* (Elm Tree Books/Hamish Hamilton, 1985) p. 78.
14. *Report of the Commission on the Constitution,* Cmnd 5460 (HMSO, 1973) I, para 231.
15. S. A. Walkland (ed.), *The House of Commons in the Twentieth Century* (Oxford University Press, 1979), p. 73.
16. Ibid.
17. *Report of the Fulton Committee on the Civil Service*, Cmnd 3638 (HMSO, 1968).
18. G. Ionescu, 'The Shrinking World of Bagehot', *Government and Opposition*, 10, no. 1 (1975) 1–11.
19. Ibid., p. 11.
20. *The Times*, 23 October 1957.
21. H. Laski, *Reflections on the Constitution* (Manchester University Press, 1951) p. 30.
22. Lord Winterton, *Orders of the Day* (Cassell, 1953), p. 42.
23. D. Butler and D. Stokes, *Political Change in Britain: Forces Shaping Electoral Choice* (Penguin, 1971) p. 509.
24. Ibid., p. 511.
25. Quoted in C. Mayhew, *Party Games* (Hutchinson, 1969), p. 167.
26. Ibid., pp. 167–8.
27. See the results as reported in J. Mackintosh (ed.), *People and Parliament* (Saxon House, 1978).
28. BBC1, 14 July 1985.
29. 'Ineffectual, Unloved, Exhausted', *Economist*, 2 Mar 1985.
30. Lord Snell, 'Daily Life in Parliament', quoted in N. Wilding and P. Laundy, *An Encyclopaedia of Parliament*, 3rd edn (Cassell, 1968) p. 461.

31. *The Times*, 22 July 1957.
32. Quoted in B. Crick, *The Reform of Parliament* (Weidenfeld and Nicolson, 1964) Appendix A, pp. 275–85.
33. Jack Straw MP, quoted in 'Life is Terrible Hard in the Stews of Westminster', *Financial Times*, 14 Feb 1982.
34. A. Mitchell, *Westminster Man: A Tribal Anthropology of the Commons People* (Methuen, 1982) p. 279.
35. Ibid., pp. 187–8.
36. Mackintosh (ed.), *People and Parliament* (Saxon House, 1978) p. 82.
37. Quoted in Mitchell, *Westminster Man*, p. 271.
38. We are grateful to Professor Charles Handy for discussing this point.
39. H. Eadie, 'The Helping Personality', *Contact*, 49 (Summer 1975) 2.
40. Ibid., p. 9.
41. L. Abse, *Private Member* (Macdonald, 1973) p. 53.
42. Lord Moran, *Winston Churchill: The Struggle for Survival, 1940–65* (Constable, 1966) *passim*.
43. D. Butler and D. Kavanagh, *The General Election of 1987* (Macmillan, 1988) p. 210.
44. R. Lewis and A. Maude, *Professional People* (Phoenix House, 1952). See also B. Barber, 'Some Problems in the Sociology of Professions', *Daedalus*, 92, no. 4 (1963); and J. A. Jackson (ed.), *Professions and Professionalization* (Cambridge University Press, 1970).
45. Walkland (ed.), *The House of Commons in the Twentieth Century*, pp. 95–96.
46. C. Mellors, *The British Member of Parliament: A Socio-Economic Survey* (Saxon House, 1978) p. 83.
47. A. King, 'The Rise of the Career Politician in Britain – and its Consequences', *British Journal of Political Science*, II, pt iii (July 1981) 250.
48. Lord Kilmuir, *Political Adventure* (Weidenfeld and Nicolson, 1964) p. 324, quoted by King in *British Journal of Political Science*, II, pt iii, p. 252.
49. O. Stevens, *Children Talking Politics* (Martin Robertson, 1982) p. 116.
50. Searing, in *Journal of Politics*, 47, p. 353.

2
Getting In

Powerful filters (political, social and legal) ensure that only certain types of individual arrive at Westminster.
(Peter Richards)

It is frequently said that the most difficult part of an MP's job is getting it in the first place. The road to Parliament is awash with the blood, sweat and tears of those who have made it – and of those who haven't. And those who haven't – at least, not the first time round – are on the increase. Between 1918 and 1955, nearly 65 per cent of all MPs were elected at their first attempt.[1] By 1974, less than half the members of the House of Commons had succeeded in their first contest and selection conferences now seem to want proof of dedication in the parade of worthy past failure. Mellors suggests that this shows that 'there is healthy competition for winnable candidatures';[2] it may also indicate the necessary single-mindedness of the long-term candidate, who, if he or she doesn't show infirmity of purpose by abandoning the race, could still end up, like Elaine Kellett-Bowman who became MP for Lancaster at her sixth attempt. Such tenacity is not often called for, and, indeed, most candidates who fail once are rewarded with a winnable seat the next time round. But more than 20 per cent of them will stand twice before getting in and some 7 per cent will try three times or more.[3]

Doing the round of constituencies, offering yourself only to be rejected, is a painful business. 'It was the most depressing period of my life!' said one who finally made it. 'I kept applying for seats, going along and meeting the same people at the selection conference and then one of us got it and the rest went away and started all over again...' Yet, before every election, several thousand candidates try for selection, and these days some 2500 actually stand.

The Boundaries Commission, which monitors demographic

changes, issued its report before the 1983 election. The result was that fifteen more constituencies were added to the previous 635. Only 650 of the election-day hopefuls, therefore, will come through with the right to put the magic letters 'MP' after their name.

DISQUALIFICATIONS AND QUALIFICATIONS

In addition to persistence, candidates have to show that they are free of certain disqualifications for membership of the House. These include infancy, lunacy, felony and bankruptcy, to which must be added, as we shall see, the holding of certain offices.[4] Sex ceased to be a disqualification (officially, at any rate) in 1918.

Officially, those under twenty-one have, since 1695, been disqualified from standing for election to the House, by the Parliamentary Elections Act of that year. Even when the age of majority was lowered to eighteen (by the Family Law Reform Act of 1969), and with it the minimum voting-age, the age of candidacy remained at twenty-one.[5]

Aliens are also disqualified from membership of the House of Commons by both common and statute law, but a naturalised British subject suffers no such disqualification.[6] Initially, common law defined aliens as all those born outside the realm and dominions, regardless of parentage, but a series of statutes, dating from the early 1700s, has progressively conferred on children of British parents born abroad, and on naturalised citizens, the same status as those born in the United Kingdom. The British Nationality Act of 1981 extended these same rights to Commonwealth citizens, and citizens of the Republic of Ireland also have the right to stand.

Almost anyone, then, can stand for Parliament, apart from the mad, the bad or peers of the realm. Those who have been certified insane are disqualified, while the Speaker also has the power, under the Mental Health Act (1959), to vacate the seat of any member who becomes insane. Imprisonment is not in itself a disqualification, but bankrupts are ineligible for five years unless they have a court certificate to show that the bankruptcy was not due to misconduct. English and Scottish peers are unable to sit in the Lower House, as they are considered to have their say in the country's affairs in their own place. Irish peers, on the other hand, do not sit in the House of Lords and may therefore be elected to the Commons. All hereditary peers can, of course, now renounce their titles under the Peerage Act of 1963, and so become eligible for Commons candidacy, or, as has more often been the case, eligible to remain in the Lower House. A peerage can only be renounced within a year of the date of succession, or, in the case of a sitting member of the House of Commons, within a month of his inheriting the title. This choice has been made by a number of MPs since 1963, including Anthony Wedgwood Benn (whose successful campaign for the right of renunciation led to the 1963 Act); Quintin Hogg, who ceased to be Lord Hailsham in 1963, only to become Lord Hailsham again, as a life peer, in 1970; and the fourteenth Earl of Home, who was able to renounce his title, return to the Commons and, as Sir Alec Douglas-Home, become Prime Minister.

Just as peers of the realm are considered to have their proper parliamentary representation in the Upper House, so the Established Church, the Church of England, is considered to be adequately represented through its bishops in the House of Lords. It may seem logical, then, that the clergy should be disqualified: yet the disqualification extends far beyond the Church of England to the Church of Scotland and that of Ireland and also to the Roman Catholic priesthood. Welsh clergy have been able to stand since the Welsh Church Act of 1914, and all nonconformist ministers can seek election. *Church and State*, the report of an Archbishops' Commission in 1970,[7] suggested that all such disqualifications should be removed and that a minister or priest of any church should be allowed to become involved in politics, but no such modifications have been made in the law. Other professional interests excluded from Commons candidature, by the House of Commons Disqualification Act of 1957, are permanent civil servants, members of the police and armed forces, judges and members of certain judicial commissions. The basis of this category of disqualification is that the number of 'offices of profit under the Crown' must be limited, otherwise a government would, in theory, be able to offer endless patronage to its supporters. Offices of profit under the Crown are therefore closed to MPs (except for the limited number of ministerial ones) and a candidate who stood while still holding such an office would be disqualified. Civil servants are, under the British system of a professional executive which does not change with changing political control, regarded as advisers to government, regardless of political persuasion. It is argued, therefore, that such advisers cannot be publicly committed to a particular political cause and still behave even-handedly with all their political masters. A civil servant then, like a policeman or soldier, who wants to stand for Parliament must first of all resign from his job.

Since members of Parliament cannot resign from the Commons, the appointment to a disqualifying office has long been the established way out for the MP who wants to go. The Stewardships of the Chiltern Hundreds and of the Manor of Northstead are used formally to disqualify members, who, on appointment, are deemed to be holders of a disqualifying office and thus unable to serve in the Commons.

The only other major disqualification affects anyone convicted under the Corrupt and Illegal Practices Prevention Act, now re-enacted in the 1949 Representation of the People Act. The fraudulent practices of a candidate or his or her agent can result in disqualification from standing in subsequent elections. Electoral fraud, although common up to the early nineteenth century, has not resulted in disqualification since 1923, when Captain Hilton-Philipson was unseated and disqualified from standing for seven years, thus bringing to the House, in the resulting by-election, only the third woman ever to sit there, his wife Mabel. Interestingly enough, of the first three women MPs, all of whom in one way or another inherited their husbands' seats, two entered the House because of their spouses' disqualification – the other being Nancy Astor, whose husband inherited his father's viscountcy and went to the Lords.

If these are the major disqualifications from candidature, the major qualifications are rather more difficult to identify. As has been said, there are no formal educational requirements or training standards, though the selection conference will expect a candidate to possess 'a good political background' or 'relevant experience'. Unlike representatives elsewhere in the world, British MPs are not required to live in the constituency for which they sit. This is something of a retreat from the position, enshrined in a statute of 1413, which required members to be resident in the county or borough they represented. The stipulation was, however, largely ignored, and it was formally repealed in 1774. In spite of this freedom to travel in order to find a seat, most MPs sit for only one constituency in the course of their parliamentary career and, indeed, a special relationship may develop between a constituency and a family, so that the link is kept over more than one generation, as happened with the Guinnesses in Southend or the Astors in Plymouth. On the other hand, the lack of a residence qualification has also allowed some members to move from a marginal to a safer seat or try to re-establish their political fortunes when they failed to see eye-to-eye with their party or their constituency. Churchill, for example, sat for no fewer than five constituencies: Oldham, Manchester North-West, Dundee, Epping and Woodford (although, of course, he did make this more likely by changing his party twice).

THE SELECTION PROCESS

Given that there are few formal requirements to be satisfied by anyone seeking to enter Parliament, and that relatively few belong to the categories automatically disqualified from candidature, the vast majority of the electorate would find that, if they so desired, they would be eligible to put themselves forward as a parliamentary hopeful. How then, would they set about this? What are the steps in the process of selection and election?

Most people who end up as parliamentary candidates begin by getting their name onto the approved list of candidates of their party. This process normally involves an interview at party headquarters, to ensure an acceptable level of political orthodoxy; and a brief investigation of background, to ensure that there are no potentially embarrassing skeletons in the candidate's cupboard. In the Conservative Party, the candidate must be proposed by two supporters, themselves Conservative MPs or peers. In the Labour Party, a candidate must be considered suitable by the National Executive Committee before she or he is put onto the approved list. The party, in fact, has not one, but two lists, designated 'A' and 'B'. The 'A' list is that composed of trade-union sponsored Labour candidates; the 'B' list consists of non-sponsored candidates. The Co-operative Party also has candidates and although it is technically a separate party, it never puts up candidates against the Labour Party and its candidates fight exclusively in the Labour interest. The process for inclusion on the approved list was similar in the Liberal Party and the SDP and is not much different in the SLD.

Getting onto the list is, however, just the first step in what may be a long and painful process – obtaining selection by a constituency; for party approval does not guarantee the chance to fight an election, never mind win a seat. What it does give is the party imprimatur, the seal of official approval, to the aspirant, who may then be sent, from time to time, information about constituencies that are seeking candidates and to which he or she may apply.

The initiative for candidate selection remains, however, not with candidates or the central headquarters of the party, but with the constituencies, which fiercely guard their independence in this respect. A constituency may approach anyone thought suitable by the local party (which generally means its officers and executive members) and such people may be asked to apply for consideration, regardless of whether they are on the approved list. Sometimes party headquarters may want to influence the choice of candidate in a constituency, but it will probably move cautiously in case it stirs up local resentment, and there are several examples of cases where the national party, keen to have a favoured candidate adopted, proceeded too directly in trying to achieve this, and offended local sensitivities to the extent of ensuring that the candidate was rejected. In 1950, for example, Lewis Silkin, the Minister of Town and Country Planning, lost his constituency when the parliamentary boundaries were redrawn. Transport House assiduously promoted his candidature with constituency after constituency, but none adopted him and he never got back into Parliament. A similar problem faced Patrick Gordon-Walker, who was made a member of the Labour Cabinet in spite of losing his seat in the 1964 election. He then lost the apparently safe seat which had been found for him and resigned immediately.

When all the applications are in, a selection committee will normally have the job of drawing up a short-list of candidates, who will then be asked to give a ten-minute speech and answer questions before a selection conference, which makes the final choice. The chosen person then becomes the prospective parliamentary candidate and can expect to fight the seat for the party in the next election. In the meantime, the candidate will be expected to 'nurse' the constituency assiduously, to build up or maintain an electoral base there, so that the electorate will come to know and recognise the person who will stand for the party at the next election.

The question of how much money it takes to be a parliamentary candidate is often raised, and some people are perhaps inhibited from seriously considering a political career because they doubt whether they will be able to afford it. It may cost a fair amount to stand in an election and it can certainly be expensive to nurse a constituency when one takes into account travel to and from the area, accommodation, support for local causes, and so on. Just before the Second World War, a Conservative candidate called Ian Harvey castigated what he called a 'plutocratic system' which resulted in the safe seats, in the Conservative Party at any rate, going to those who could afford to pay their own election expenses and contribute to party funds.[8] Since the Maxwell Fyfe Report, however, the amount a candidate can contribute to party funds has been strictly controlled at a modest level, and all election expenses are met by the party and not by the candidate. This is true in all the main parties now, and, although it may still cost money to pursue a political career, to be on the spot and act and dress the part, the expense of keeping the party show on the road is no longer seen as the candidate's responsibility.

In the Labour Party, the situation is complicated somewhat by the existence of union sponsorship. However, the amount a union can contribute in any particular constituency is strictly limited. In some constituencies, the Labour candiate will be supported by a union which will provide a small amount of financial backing and perhaps an agent or other services for the candidate. The number of sponsored candidates does not seem to be falling. In 1945, there were 125 of them;[9] by 1987, the number was 184.[10] There is invariably a high success rate among sponsored candidates, as they tend to be in seats with safe Labour majorities, and around 70–75 per cent of them are generally returned to the Commons, where they make up around a third of all Labour MPs. In 1983, for example, when Labour suffered badly at the polls, it was the union-sponsored candidates who held on most successfully to their seats, and well over half of all Labour members returned were sponsored.

THE ELECTION OF THE MEMBER

Finally, when the day of the election comes, voters will be asked to choose one candidate only from amongst those standing. The candidates' names used to appear without their party affiliation on the ballot paper, and much was often made of the fact that the British, eccentric but politically astute as ever, managed to conduct elections without so much as a mention of political parties. This, apparently, had the advantage of avoiding complicated rules 'about what constitutes a political party, about how parties should be organised, or about how they should nominate candidates'.[11] The main disadvantage here was that people vote more for parties than for individual candidates, and the possibility of putting your cross, in ignorance, against the wrong name was high. Perhaps it was a further indication of British political genius that, when the rules were changed and name and party appeared together on the ballot paper, no complex legal problems arose and the only result was that more of the electorate were now confident that they knew for whom they were voting.

The British electoral system is of the single-member, first-past-the-post variety. That is, the one individual who polls the highest number of votes in a constituency wins the seat. There is no proportionality as between votes and seats; it is 'winner takes all'. As we shall see, this may have implications for the type of candidate selected. It also makes British elections peculiarly exciting and immediate affairs. The votes are counted manually, growing in individual piles for the various candidates, and, when the winner has been identified, the result is announced, in most cases within a few hours of the close of the polls. There is no working-out of complicated formulas to determine shares of the vote locally or nationally before the outcome can be known. The contestant quickly knows whether he or she has been successful, in which case the next stop is Westminster, or if not, the selection round may have to be faced all over again. If the candidate has not managed to secure at least one eighth of the votes cast, he or she will lose the deposit, now £500, which has to be lodged by all those standing, its purpose being to deter frivolous candidatures. If the candidate has increased the party's share of the vote, even if the seat has not been won, he or she will probably be sought by the constituency again as its candidate; but all prospective parliamentary candidates resign after an election and anyone who has done reasonably well for the party may feel due a safer seat next time round. After all, the odds suggest better luck then.

ROUTES TO PARLIAMENT

Turning from candidates to members, it is clear that the pathways to Parliament are well-trodden ones. There is much that is common to the backgrounds and experience of MPs of all political parties. First, very many of them come from families with strong traditional political connections. The Churchills, Guinnesses, Devonshires and so on are only the most obvious and enduring political dynasties; but the Commons in recent years has been full of young, and not so young, men, and occasionally women, who have had family there. Tony Benn, David Marquand, Adam Butler, Shirley Summerskill, John (and Sam) Silkin, Douglas Hogg, Michael Foot – the list is long and distinguished. When one thinks how much of a minority interest politics is, it is perhaps not surprising that an addiction to it is very often an inherited condition. From parents and other close relations, people acquire a sense of priorities and a sense of possibilities; politics is a learned reaction, and those who have been brought up with it acquire not only information and the techniques of the game, but also the belief that the game itself is worth playing. Politics is legitimised for them; they believe that they can affect events as their parents have done before them, and that political involvement is a worthy and not a corrupt enterprise. David Marquand, for example, hardly starry-eyed after his journalistic experience, yet with the background of a politician father, still believed that 'sitting writing editorials in the corridor of the old *Guardian* building in Manchester was rather too lazy a way of expressing one's views and one really ought to be a bit more committed and a bit more active'.[12] Someone from a different background might well have thought otherwise.

Most MPs, regardless of family connections, arrive in Parliament by one of two or three main routes. Local government is one such training-ground; the local and national party is another; and in the Labour Party the trade unions can also provide experience and a power base for politically ambitious individuals. Local government has always produced a fair number of national aspirants who have been able to use the experience they gained as councillors to launch themselves into the wider political sphere. Not that by any means all local politicians have national aspirations. For many, the local scene is what they enjoy, either because they see it as more relevant or because they do not have the self-confidence to try to join the big league. Many local politicians too, especially those who are involved in large urban councils, feel they have more power at this level than they would ever have as a backbench MP. Some who have gone to Westminster echo this belief; Millie Miller, for example, was convinced that during her short stay at Westminster she had considerably less power than when she was mayor of Stoke Newington and leader of Camden Borough Council.[13] In similar vein, Ruth Dalton was brutally frank to Ramsay MacDonald when he inquired why she was returning from the House to the London County Council: 'There they do things', she said; 'here we just talk.'

None the less, for many MPs, local government is their political apprenticeship. This has always been so in the Labour Party, and many of the great Labour leaders, such as Clement Attlee, Herbert Morrison and George Lansbury, assiduously maintained their local government roots. Indeed, at every general election, apart from 1959 and 1979, more than 40 per cent of all Labour MPs have come from this background.[14] In 1983, the highest ever proportion, 47.8 per cent, was recorded, and when *new* Labour MPs, as opposed to *all* Labour MPs, are considered, nearly 65 per cent of them had local government experience.[15] In the Conservative Party, this background has always been less common. It may be that Conservative MPs have tended to come from business or service backgrounds, which sit less easily with local government demands, or simply that their more confident social and educational backgrounds allowed them to go straight to the parliamentary level of politics. At any rate, in 1945, only 14.1 per cent of all Conservative MPs had served as members of local authorities.[16] By 1983, however, that figure had risen to 38.1 per cent, and, when new members only are considered, 52 per cent are found to have a local government background.[17] Local government then, appears to be on the increase as a testing-ground for the national scene, and more politicians than not, regardless of party, get their experience in this arena.

The local party may also be an important stepping-stone on the way to Parliament. For many, of course, local party and local government go hand in hand; some, however, eschew local government as 'parish-pump politics' and decide to make the local and then the national party the jumping-off point. If this route is chosen, the aspiring member will probably try to become an office-holder in the constituency party and, in so doing, both show willing and become known. At the same time, the experience is invaluable to many people who would not otherwise have the chance to learn to speak in public, bone up on party philosophy and assimilate the basics of committee mores.

The importance of union sponsorship has already been mentioned. Although a high proportion of Labour MPs are union-backed, these people need not necessarily have much relation to the sponsoring union. What made John Silkin a likely member of the Transport and General Workers, for example? And Old Etonian Tam Dalyell would probably not immediately come to mind as the obvious choice of the National Union of Railwaymen. On the other hand, the National Union of Mineworkers normally only supports miners, and the Amalgamated Union of Engineering Workers is faithful to its own products, thus keeping open a route to the Commons for working-class representatives who might be unlikely to have either the experience or the incentive to come in any other way.

SOCIAL AND EDUCATIONAL BACKGROUNDS OF MPS

This latter point raised the whole question of the social and educational backgrounds of MPs. It has been claimed recently that the class background of members has changed in a number of ways. Labour MPs, it is said, are no longer of working-class origin; politics, regardless of party affiliation, is a largely middle-class pursuit. It was not always so, however, and it is estimated that in 1918 87 per cent of the membership of the Parliamentary Labour Party came from a working-class background.[18] The proportion fell more or less progressively – a reflection, perhaps, of changes in the composition of the labour force and therefore of the class backgrounds of Labour supporters and activists. Even between 1950 and 1965, for example, there was a fall of 5 per cent in the proportion of the workforce engaged in manual occupations.[19] A recent study suggests that this 'shrinking' of the working class is even more dramatic – from 47 per cent of the electorate in 1964 to 34 per cent in 1983.[20] Whatever the reasons, the decline in the number of manual workers in the House went with an increase in the proportion of MPs with a university education and, in the Labour Party, with a continuous rise in the proportion of MPs drawn from the teaching and lecturing professions. By 1966, the proportion of what Butler calls 'rank-and-file' workers among Labour MPs was about 30 per cent, as opposed to 72 per cent in the inter-war period, while the proportion with a university education increased from 15 per cent to 51 per cent.[21] It looked as if MPs of all parties were becoming increasingly similar in background and experience.

Yet the proportion of middle-class professionals among new Labour MPs in 1983 was down, and the proportion of manual workers was up (marginally, to about 20 per cent). At a time of great uncertainty for the Labour Party – in 1983 the number of Labour MPs reached its lowest level since 1935 – this may not indicate an established change, but Burch and Moran, in their article on the British political elite, claim that the 'trend towards an increasingly middle-class, white-collar, professional party does . . . appear to have slowed down in 1979 and by 1983 may even have been reversed'.[22] The 1987 results showed only a levelling off, with almost identical proportions of professionals and manual workers as in 1983. However, the suggestion of a move towards a greater working-class representation in the parliamentary Labour Party is intriguing, as it flies in the face of the conventional wisdom of almost all post-war political sociology, which leans heavily on theories of 'embourgoisement' and the 'professionalisation' of politics, and generally argues that a meritocratic system will throw up politicians of essentially similar type – middle-class, highly educated professionals – regardless of party. Burch and Moran are wise to be tentative about their findings here. As they admit, the developments they chronicle are not confirmed even over two election intakes. Again, it is clearly much too early for those who have been embarrassed by the preponderance of the middle-class in the Parliamentary Labour Party to rejoice, and, even if the trend were to continue, the reasons for it might prove less than palatable. Why, for example, was there a 'marked decline in those [Labour MPs] with professional occupations in 1983'?[23] Is it due to a welcome broadening of the base of the activist involvement or simply a reflection of the belief of ambitious professional people that their chances of political success in the Labour Party are now much diminished, so leading them to opt out of candidature and leave room for the non-professionals? Clearly, it may take several more elections before such questions can be answered.

If the composition of the Parliamentary Labour Party has changed somewhat over the past few years, so too has that of the

Conservatives, and perhaps less ambiguously than in the case of its socialist rival. In the period from 1945 to 1974, the party largely maintained what Mellors calls the 'patrician tradition': public school and Oxbridge were the common background of approaching 50 per cent of Conservative members over this period.[24] Up to 1974, 'the old school tie remain[ed] the most important qualification available to prospective Conservative MPs.... As a guarantee of electoral success it ranks with the reliability afforded by sponsorship from the mineworkers' union in the Labour party.'[25] Between 1979 and 1987, however, significant changes seemed to take place. The proportion of public school-boys, for example, fell from 73 per cent in 1979 to 64 per cent in 1983.[26] If only new MPs are considered, the fall is even more dramatic, from 87 per cent in 1974 to 53 per cent in 1979 and again to 47 per cent in 1983.[27] Over the same period, the percentage of new members with a public school and Oxbridge background fell from just over 62 per cent to 25 per cent, and in 1987, for the third election in a row, the number of Conservative Etonians declined (to 43).[28]

It has become fashionable, particularly since 1983, to denigrate the quality of the new Conservative members. Julian Critchley recalls the horror with which an older backbencher castigated him in the fifties for 'wearin' suede shoes'; 'Now', remarks Critchley lugubriously, 'we're all wearing suede shoes.' The clear implication is that the tone of the party, its social level, has dropped. The same point is made, none too subtly, by Bernard Levin, who remarks that 'many new Tory MPs look, sound and behave like used-car salesmen'.[29] Tendentious such comments may be, but they do reflect a certain reality; for, although some of the changes in recruitment to the party may be due to the extraordinary Conservative majorities of 1979 and, especially, 1983, which, as one older member suggested, 'brought people into the House who were never expected to get there', still this cannot be the whole story. As Burch and Moran show, it is not just in the marginal seats, which the party might not have been expected to win, that the profile of Conservative members has changed. In the thirty-two safest Conservative seats, they found that, rather than being 'dominated by well-connected patricians ... this group contains exactly the same proportion of public school/Oxbridge products as among the MPs as a whole, while the proportion of Old Etonians and public school products are almost identical in the two groups'.[30] In view of such evidence, it is hard not to agree that the backgrounds of Conservative candidates and MPs has changed significantly, and probably permanently, over the past few years.

It is, of course, easier to trace and characterise the backgrounds of candidates in the two larger parties than in the Alliance or the SLD. This is because there are no historical data for the latter before the 1983 election, unless comparison is made simply with the Liberals, and, even then, the very small number of Liberals in the post-war period makes it impossible to produce meaningful figures in this context. What can be said with some certainty is that their parliamentary membership is overwhelmingly middle-class, highly educated and professional – much the same, in fact, as the two other parties.[31]

While it may take more evidence over a longer period to establish conclusive changes in the class and educational backgrounds of members, the emergence of the 'professional' politician is well-documented and generally accepted. Buck, in his study, suggests that an MP becomes a professional on winning his third election.[32] Mellors defines the professional as the member serving ten years or more in the House and goes on to show that the number so doing has significantly increased since the war. In 1945, the average length of service was just over five years; in 1974, it was ten years.[33] Politics has become for most MPs a full-time profession which they enter and intend, the electorate willing, to remain in all their working lives. Such a full-time professional, says Bernard Crick, 'is a natural response to the volume and complexities of modern legislation'.[34] This may well be true, but there are those who believe it is not a costless process. As Anthony King describes him, the 'career politician' is to be recognised not merely by his long and devoted service, or by his specialist, professional approach, but also by his attitude. 'With the rise of the career politician, there has also occurred a rise in the incidence of political ambition.'[35] And, although it is such ambitious individuals who may generally make the greatest contributions to politics because of their acquired experience, assertion and self-confidence, yet 'they have had less experience of the world outside politics than their predecessors, and they show signs of being more partisan, more doctrinaire and less in touch with the mass electorate'. In short, the rise of the career politician may have meant greater efficiency, ambition and expertise, but it has also 'led to a certain loss of experience, moderation, detachment, balance, ballast even, in the British political system'.[36]

THE REPRESENTATION OF WOMEN AND ETHNIC MINORITIES

Members of Parliament are typically middle-class, middle-aged and male. They are also almost all white. The apparent inability of the system to select substantial numbers of black or female candidates is currently much discussed. Women, who make up some 52 per cent of the electorate, have never composed more than 6 per cent of the House of Commons and that only for the first time in 1987. Black candidates have fared even worse. Yet in 1892 Dadabhai Naoroji, an Indian, won Finsbury Central for the Liberals and was the first non-white to be elected. He was followed by Sir Mancherjee Bhownagree, who sat as a Conservative in 1895 and again in 1900. A third Indian, Shapurji Saklatvala, was elected Labour member for Battersea North in 1922 and again in the same constituency, as a Communist, in 1924. For the next sixty years, however, in spite of a substantial rise in the number of black citizens, no black candidates at all were elected. It was not until 1987 that four black MPs entered the House, all representing the Labour Party.

In the case of women, they have had the right to stand for the House of Commons since 1918, and the first woman member, Nancy Astor, was elected in a by-election in 1919. Since then, there have always been women in Parliament, but only in penny numbers and with little cumulative reflection of women's changing role in society. Since the Second World War, the variation in representation has been slight: between a low of 2.7 per cent in 1951 and a high of 6.3 per cent in 1987.[37] Thus, although sex and colour are not legal or official disqualifications from membership of the House, they are clearly handicaps. In 1983, for example, a white man's chance of election, once selected, was between one in three and one in four; a woman's was one in twelve and a black candidate evidently had no chance at all. The question then becomes, do women and blacks make bad candidates? Does the electorate reject them because of this or do those who select candidates discriminate against them? It is possible, of course, that the answer lies in a combination of all these factors and that the answer is different for the two groups.

As far as women are concerned, there is no evidence that they are bad candidates or that the electorate rejects them. Indeed, it seems that most people still support a party rather than an individual, and research shows that, where a man and a woman are standing in equivalent seats, there is little to choose between their performances at the polls and, as Hills says, 'overall the general differences in success are negligible'.[38] The electorate, it appears, does not discriminate against women; rather the problem comes at the point of the selection of candidates. Women are disproportionately selected for the unwinnable or marginal seats and by the minority parties. Charlot claims that, in 1979, the Conservatives gave only one of their 191 safe seats to a woman, while the Labour Party gave only eight of their 209. Further, nearly half the Conservative and over a third of the Labour women who stood did so in seats which were absolutely safe – for the opposition.[39] In 1983, the concept of a 'safe seat' was more difficult to determine, partly because of the emergence of the Alliance and partly because the redistribution of seats produced, in some cases, new parliamentary constituencies. Just before the election, however, Labour reckoned that only 25 of its 78 women candidates were in seats which were 'winnable'. In the event, only ten won. On the Conservative side, only about 20 women were in seats thought by the party to be winnable and, even with a landslide victory, only 13 got in.[40]

It is notable that when women achieved a rather higher representation after the 1987 election, it was as a result of more women candidates being selected for safe or winnable seats. In the Labour Party, for example, three women were selected for traditionally working-class, male bastions of the North-East: Durham, Redcar and Gateshead. Women also ran in safe London, Bristol and Glasgow seats. The Conservatives selected four new women for safe seats in Devon West, Billericay, Maidstone and Norfolk. It was consequently clear before the election that, almost regardless of the overall result, between 39 and 41 women would enter the House.

It has been argued that there is no evidence that women are discriminated against by selectors, and one piece of research suggests that Labour selectors, at any rate, are not unsupportive of women.[41] However, since selectors were asked directly if, other things being equal, constituency Labour parties should select more women, it may be that the response was simply a claim to be against sin rather than anything more positively favourable to women. It is also hardly encouraging that, in view of the rather anodyne wording, with its *ceterus paribus* addition, only 60 per cent answered 'yes' to the question. It is difficult to resist Max Morris's conclusion that, in the Labour Party at least, 'when the chips are down and the scramble for seats is on, the hard left seems to prefer white, Anglo-Saxon males'.[42] Not that the position is much better in the Conservative Party, where in 1987 only about 7 per cent of candidates were women (as against 14.5 per cent for Labour, and 16.5 per cent for the Alliance). However, the impact of a female leader may have been felt on the collective consciousness of the party if a poll taken in February 1983 is anything to go by. People were asked if they thought women should have a greater role in the running of the country. 75 per cent of Conservative voters said yes and only 18 per cent no. The Alliance response was almost identical (74 per cent in favour, 19 per cent against), but only 63 per cent of Labour voters wanted women to be more involved, while 32 per cent did not.[43] In the same poll, voters were asked if they thought that men were better fitted than women to be MPs. Again, only 33 per cent of Conservatives but 45 per cent of Labour voters (32 per cent Alliance) agreed with this. If Labour selectors are disinclined to select women because they fear the electorate will not support a female candidate, these figures may give them some support. Nevertheless, it was in one of Labour's safe seats, Hackney North, that the constituency party in December 1985 selected Diane Abbott as its parliamentary candidate, ensuring that she would become in 1987 the first black woman to sit in the House.

While the arguments about women candidates abound, those about black candidates become more and more bitter. Many black candidates feel that they are simply not given the chance to stand and that selectors are deeply suspicious of their ability to deliver the vote. There is some evidence that, whereas women candidates are not a significant disincentive to electoral support, black candidates may be. When Dr David Pitt (now Lord Pitt) fought Clapham for Labour in 1970, it was thought to be winnable, but he lost the seat with a swing of more than 10 per cent against him, when neighbouring seats were moving to the Conservatives by only 2 or 3 per cent. The belief that black candidates lose white votes is still widely held and is supported by some empirical evidence.[44] In some constituencies, however, there is now a heavy concentration of ethnic minorities. In 16 parliamentary constituencies, they make up more than 30 per cent of the population, and in another 37 constituencies more than 20 per cent.[45] Courting the ethnic vote therefore becomes a political prority, and indeed the Conservative Party estimated that, in 1987, in some 30 marginals the ethnic vote was larger than the existing majority and could therefore, in theory, decide the seat.

It may also be the case that being black is no longer such a handicap as it was, especially in certain parts of the country. London, for example, had by 1987 over 70 black councillors, who were both gaining relevant political experience and accustoming the electorate to black leadership. In the 1983 general election, the swing away from the black Labour Party candidate in Westminster South, Russell Profitt, was 7.3 per cent, which compared very favourably with the inner-London average of 7.1 per cent.[46] By 1987 three black Labour candidates, Paul Boateng (Brent South), Bernie Grant (Tottenham) and Diane Abbott were chosen for winnable London seats, and Keith Vaz for Leicester East. All went on to the House after the general election.

The representation of women and black people is, however, proportionally very low. In this context, the argument is sometimes made that a proportional electoral system would be likely to increase the representation of women and of candidates from the ethnic communities. Under the present single-member, first-past-the-post system, the tendency is for those who selected candidates to choose the one individual who looks likely to maximise the vote. In almost all cases, this is liable to be the kind of candidate who has won elections in the past – the standard product, a middle-class, middle-aged, white male. There is, then, under the single-member system, little incentive to look further than this, and women and black candidates are consequently at a disadvantage in obtaining selection. In proportional systems the political pressure is again to maximise the appeal of candidates to the votes, but here the parties normally present the electors with a list of candidates, rather than one name per party per constituency. The incentive for selectors is therefore to present a balanced list, appealing as widely as possible to voters, and it would probably be a politically inept move to present a list bereft of women to an electorate over half of which is female. As Vernon Bogdanor points out, whereas under the single-member system it is the presence of a candidate who deviates from the (male) norm which is noticed, in a list system it would be the absence of women (or, in certain constituencies, of black candidates), the failure to present a balanced ticket, that would be obvious.[47]

For Parliament to be proportionately representative of the black community, there would have to be around 25 black MPs, while for women the figure would, of course, be in excess of 325. These numbers are most unlikely to be achieved in the near future – or ever, some would say. Strict proportionality may be unnecessary, but, while gross anomalies exist and some elements of the community feel excluded from the House of Commons – which is, after all, the central representative institution of British democracy – the political process is itself far from secure. In such a context, the job of the representative, already in question, may be further devalued.

NOTES

1. P. Buck, *Amateurs and Professionals in Politics* (Chicago University Press, 1963), p. 96.
2. C. Mellors, *The British Member of Parliament: A Socio-Economic Survey* (Saxon House, 1978) p. 25.
3. Data derived from *The Times Guide to the House of Commons* (Times Newspapers) 1979, 1983.
4. N. Wilding and Laundy, *An Encyclopaedia of Parliament*, 3rd edn (Cassell, 1968), p. 204.
5. *Family Law Reform Act* 1969, Schedule 2, para 2.
6. See Sir Thomas Erskine May, *Parliamentary Practice*, 20th edn, ed. Sir Charles Gordon (Butterworth, 1983) p. 39.
7. The report was published by the Church Information Office.
8. Part of Harvey's memorandum is reproduced in an appendix to J. F. S. Ross, *Parliamentary Representation* (Eyre and Spottiswoode, 1943).
9. P. G. Richards, *Honourable Members* (Faber and Faber, 1959) p. 2.
10. Figures from Transport House. See also D. Butler and J. Kavanagh, *The General Election of 1987* (Macmillan, 1988) p. 206.
11. A. H. Birch, *The British System of Government*, 2nd edn. (Allen and Unwin, 1968) p. 82.
12. Quoted in A. Mitchell, *Westminster Man: A Tribal Anthropology of the Commons People* (Methuen, 1982) p. 26.
13. See E. Vallance, *Women in the House: A Study of Women MPs* (Athlone Press, 1979) p. 29.
14. Mellors, *The British MP*, p. 91.
15. M. Burch and M. Moran,' The Changing British Political Elite, 1945–1983: MPs and Cabinet Ministers', *Parliamentary Affairs*, 38, no. 1 (1985) 14.
16. Mellors, *The British MP*, p. 91.
17. Burch and Moran, in *Parliamentary Affairs*, 38, no. 1, pp. 13–14.
18. W. L. Guttsman, 'The British Political Elite and the Class Structure', in P. Stanworth and A. Giddens (eds), *Elites and Power in British Society* (Cambridge University Press, 1974) p. 33.
19. See R. Knight, 'Changes in the Occupational Structure of the Working Population', *Journal of the Royal Statistical Society*, 1967, pp. 408–22.
20. A. Heath *et al.*, *How Britain Votes*, (Pergamon, 1985) p. 36; See also S. E. Finch 'The Mystery of Labour's Lost Voters', *The Times Higher Education Supplement*, 13 Dec 1985.

21. D. Butler and D. Stokes, *Political Change in Britain* (Penguin, 1966) p. 153.
22. Burch and Moran, in *Parliamentary Affairs*, 38, no. 1, p. 8.
23. Ibid.
24. Mellors, *The British MP*, p. 47.
25. Ibid.
26. Burch and Moran, in *Parliamentary Affairs*, 38, no. 1, p. 13.
27. Ibid., p. 14.
28. Butler and Kavanagh, *The British General Election of 1987*, p. 201.
29. *The Times*, 21 May 1985.
30. Burch and Moran, in *Parliamentary Affairs*, 38, no. 1, p. 6.
31. Information derived from *The Times Guide to the House of Commons*, 1983.
32. Buck, *Amateurs and Professionals in British Politics*, p. 132.
33. Mellors, *The British MP*, p. 87.
34. B. Crick, *The Reform of Parliament* (Weidenfeld and Nicolson, 1964) p. 55. Quoted in Mellors, *The British MP*, p. 124.
35. A. King, 'The Rise of the Career Politician in Britain – and its Consequences', *British Journal of Political Science*, II, pt iii (July 1981) 250.
36. Ibid., p. 285.
37. E. Vallance, 'Two Cheers for Equality: Women Candidates in the 1987 General Election', *Parliamentary Affairs*, 41, no. 1 (1988) 86.
38. J. Hills, 'Candidates: The Impact of Gender', *Parliamentary Affairs*, 34, no. 2 (1981) 228. See also E. Vallance, 'Women Candidates and Elector Preference', *Politics*, 1, no. 2 (1981).
39. M. Charlot, 'Women and Elections in Britain', in H. Pennman (ed.), *The General Election of 1979* (American Enterprise Institute for Public Policy, 1981) p. 253.
40. See E. Vallance, 'Women Candidates in the 1983 General Election', *Parliamentary Affairs*, 37, no. 3 (1984) 305.
41. J. Bochel and D. Denver, 'Candidate Selection in the Labour Party: What the Selectors Seek', *British Journal of Political Science*, 13, no. 1 (1983) 55.
42. 'The Other Way that Labour isn't Working', *Guardian*, 25 Feb 1983.
43. Marplan poll conducted for the *Guardian*, Feb 1983 (question 15).
44. See M. Steed, 'The Results Analysed', in D. Butler and D. Kavanagh, *The British General Election of February 1974* (Macmillan, 1974) p. 335.
45. *The Times*, 18 Mar 1983.
46. Ibid.
47. V. Bogdanor, *What is Proportional Representation? (Martin Robertson, 1984) p. 115. See also E. Lakeman, Power to Elect* (Heinemann, 1982) ch. 8.

3

The Job in Parliament

*The average MP works at greater
pressure and for longer hours than
nine-tenths of those who elect
him. . . .*

(Lord Snell)

It is a life of great frustration.
(Mr Speaker Weatherill)

After the uncertainties of selection and the hectic activity of
election, when the adrenalin has ceased pumping, the excitement
of the television cameras at St Stephen's entrance has passed, and
the anti-climax of the swearing-in ceremony has come and gone,
what do the new Members of Parliament actually do? The first
hurdle which looms, the maiden speech, is in many ways indicative of the life which follows. Most members try to get it out of the
way as soon as possible, but there is no necessity to do so. There
are traditions surrounding it, comforting to cling to but not
mandatory, and certainly not always respected. In this, as in so
much else to do with the job, it is almost entirely up to individual
members, once installed, what they do and when and how they do
it. They need not even take up their seat once won, though they
will not get paid if they decline to take the oath of office. There are,
however, no penalties for non-attendance such as exist in other
parliaments, even those based on the Westminster model. The
ultimate sanction is simply that of not being elected next time. For
those who want to stay in the job, an important consideration must
be the need to retain the confidence of the party and the constituency, and, particularly in these days of reselection, of the party
in the constituency, but most members' work patterns do not
necessarily derive purely from such motivations. Much of what
members do will be reactive, influenced by events in the world at
large, by party policy, the government's programme and consti-

tuency concerns; but much will also depend on their own interests and enthusiasms; and how much they do will depend on their consciences, their willingness to meet the demands of the party whips, and their energy levels. 'The job is infinitely expandable' says Alan Amos MP. 'Politicians set their own level of work', adds Bryan Gould MP; 'if they are conscientious and ambitious, then obviously their workload is heavier.' If they are neither, they can, equally, get away with doing comparatively little, especially if they do not care whether they are re-elected or have decided not to stand again.

Much though some members have wished for it, there is no clear or detailed job description. In the opinion of Dennis Canavan MP, 'The role of the MP is to fight for the interests of the people you represent on local and national matters.' There may be additional agendas. For Paul Boateng, as a black member, there is the added 'privilege and responsibility' of 'gaining respect in terms of Parliamentary and Committee work reflecting that a multiracial society exists and what it can achieve.' The only statement of what their job might be which is broadly agreed by members themselves is daunting in its scope: 'to represent, defend and promote national interests; and further the needs and interests of constituents, reconciling them with national interests so far as possible'. This description was devised by Hay Management Consultants, advising the Top Salaries Review Body chaired by Lord Plowden. The TSRB reports remain a valuable quarry of information on members' jobs, pay and allowances, much drawn upon in this and subsequent chapters.[1] The TSRB definition highlights appropriately the duality of members' jobs, their responsibility to the constituents who elect them, and to the nation as a whole in Parliament. Each can be a full-time occupation in itself. New members are confronted with choices and a range of possible roles within which they must make their own priorities. In effect, they are given, as one described it, 'a build your own job kit . . . and left to get on with it'. They have won by their election not so much a career as 'access to a tangle of wires and levers, some to push and some to pull'.[2]

It is hardly surprising then, to find newcomers to Westminster bemused and confused as they embark on their lives as honourable members. Some are lucky to have the guidance of friends and colleagues already in the House, or are familiar with its procedures and geography, like Alan Amos, who had studied Parliament, taught it, and frequented it in the course of working in the

Conservative Research Department, and Hilary Armstrong, who as a student in London had often visited her MP father there. A number arrive, however, confessing like Gillian Shephard, to 'unplumbable ignorance' of the workings of Parliament, and like Keith Vaz, having never seen a Whip, with no idea of what 'tabling' a motion meant, and finding 'there was no-one to ask'. The introduction and orientation most receive when they first arrive is frequently described as 'totally inadequate'. 'There is no seminar to introduce new members to the geography of the House', Michael Hirst recalled, 'nobody takes you round, nobody shows you where things are, nobody explains procedures to you, tells you what an early-day motion is about and so on.' Still less does anyone instruct or guide the new members on how they should do their jobs beyond the semi-jocular generalities such as 'specialise and stay out of the bars'. More could be done. Members receive only a daunting, impersonal folder of information about financial arrangements and the functions of the various Departments of the House, a short explanation from the Clerks about how to put down questions, and a video and conducted tour of the Library. Outside organisations have attempted to fill the breach; the Centre for Advanced Urban Studies has run introductory seminars for new members, and the Royal Institute of Public Administration has offered them useful courses on 'The Workings of Whitehall'.

Detailed and specific guidance would be difficult to provide, for the fact is that in every Parliament there are at least 650 ways of doing the job of an MP. All MPs have the same basic components in their 'job kit' – Parliament, the constituency, party commitments and so on – but they combine the different shapes and the different parts of these major components to produce an amazing variety of patterns, almost like a kaleidoscope. The result is that generalisations about MPs and talk about the 'average' are more or less meaningless. As John Biffen (who spoke as Leader of the House, and might be expected to know) put it, 'There is no such thing as an average Member of Parliament. That is an abstract concept. We have ... 650 people who adopt completely different approaches to work.'[3]

COMPONENTS OF THE JOB

The differences between MPs' styles and the kinds of jobs they construct start with their constituencies, which, as Hay points out, exercise a powerful influence on the nature of the working-life that members devise for themselves. There is wide variation between constituencies, which average 150 square miles and 65,000 constituents, and have an average economic activity level of £420 million a year.[4] Variables such as economic conditions, predominating industries, types and levels of employment, size, topography and whether the area is predominantly urban or rural will help shape the kind of jobs members find themselves doing, and dictate some priorities, even before the member's own personality, preferences and perceptions are brought to bear. Distance from Westminster alone ensures that a member with a constituency in the south-east of England will have a rather different work pattern from a colleague who represents a constituency in Scotland, the south-west or Northern Ireland. A scattered constituency will make different demands on its members from an inner-city area, both in terms of travel within the constituency and in terms of the likely preoccupations and problems of the people there. The job of Alexander Pollock, with the sparsely populated Scottish constituency of Moray, covering some 700 square miles, will necessarily differ in very many respects from the job done by Diane Abbott, the black Labour member for London's Hackney and Stoke Newington. Members dealing with socio-economically deprived areas are likely to find themselves heavily embroiled in untangling problems relating to social security, housing and welfare. On the other hand, members with affluent rural constituencies are likely to have to respond mostly to quite different demands – for example, for reasoned responses on questions of domestic or foreign policy.

Political factors are also important in shaping MPs' jobs. A slim majority in the constituency will probably mean a larger proportion of time has to be spent there, nursing it, than otherwise. Again, even the job done by the same member for the same constituency may differ in different Parliaments, depending on whether his or her party is in government or opposition. A small government majority in the House may well entail long, late sittings and few nights off, with heavy demands on both government and opposition MPs but particularly on the former, whose whips will be anxious to retain their lead in the division lobbies. The small number of Independent members, and those from the often locally based opposition parties, such as the Scottish National Party or

Plaid Cymru, may well have to spend a greater than average time away from Westminster, nursing the constituency or promoting the party and cultivating the grass roots.

These constituency and political variables which shape the job will also be amplified by personal factors, relating to the member's personality, circumstances and preferences. Length of service in the House may be significant. An experienced member with a specialism, the respect of his colleagues and knowledge of how to work the levers of power and influence will do a different job from the newer member, whose energy, enthusiasm and iconoclastic attitudes to traditional parliamentary mores may also be productive. Members with special interests, experience and knowledge will probably want to use them. Those maintaining professional commitments outside the House will tend to spend less time in the Palace of Westminster than those without such involvements. Those with families and a main home in London will probably have a different working-pattern from those with no domestic commitments, or those who have family as well as professional reasons for spending time in the constituency. Variables of this sort that are likely to influence the shape of an MP's job are legion, even before strategic decisions about priorities within the broad scope of the work are broached.

Members themselves, as well as observers of Parliament, have widely differing philosophies about what their priorities should be. Hay usefully identifies the range of tasks MPs might have to perform and the roles they might have to play if the job, however one defines it, is to be acceptably executed in Westminster, the constituency and the party. Members, Hay says, have to form the pool of personnel from which government and opposition are formed; they monitor and challenge governments in order to influence them in 'desirable' ways; they 'initiate, amend and review legislation'; they help maintain a 'continually relevant and appropriate body of law'; they further the interests of both constituents and the constituency; contribute to the formation of party policy; and contribute to the dissemination and achievement of that policy.[5]

Plainly it is hard for members to find the time, or energy, to be all these things at once, even if they have the requisite skills, although most probably attempt some of them, with varying degrees of success at one time or another. Perhaps the major choice for most members, whether consciously made or not, is where they strike the balance between constituency and parliamentary work; whether, that is, they gain a reputation as a 'good constituency member', or aim for high office and a name in the House itself.

Most new backbenchers, when interviewed, do tend to see themselves as 'good constituency MPs', both because they themselves feel this is their most important role, and because their constituents often see this as central to the job. Norton has noted that constituency MPs have little time for specialisation, given their immersion in the complexities of cases which demand general rather than specific skills.[6] Donald Searing has further subdivided constituency MPs into two different categories – the 'welfare officers' and the 'local promoters'.[7] The latter see themselves largely as putting forward local and regional interests (as, say, spokesman for the textile industry or the north-east region) rather than acting only on behalf of individual constituents. Of the constituency members, the majority, however, see themselves as welfare officers, 'shouting', as Searing put it, 'for constituents' needs rather than for their political opinions. And they shout where they are most likely to be heard – at Westminster. This pleases their constituents, since this is what their constituents believe they should be doing. This also helps to check the executive, since when they shout at Westminster, administrators become more sensitive to possible errors or injustices than they would otherwise be.'[8]

The role of constituency MP gives members of Parliament a sense of their own competence as well as providing them with the psychological satisfaction of a duty fulfilled. Though modern backbenchers are, at one level, simply carrying on the traditional parliamentary function of redress of grievances, the issues are now more complex. As one member says,

> I think probably the most important thing of all is to serve as a brake on, and as a warning to, bureaucracy. That to my mind is the greatest importance of the constituency system. Everybody in this country has got an MP to go to and it's his job to take their protest, if it's a good one, right to the top. And every bureaucrat in the town hall and the local government office is subject to the quite considerable threat: 'If they behave like this, I'll go and see my MP' – that's very important. You have got to have an awful lot of government in an advanced society. And the great danger is the tyranny of the bureaucrat. We are the limitation on the tyranny'.[9]

'Career politicians' or 'ministerial aspirants' are, according to Anthony King, a relatively new breed of men and women.[10] The characteristics which distinguish them are political determination, an early start in politics and therefore entry to Parliament at a young age, and a relatively late retirement. The growth in the number of career politicians reflects fairly recent trends in government where members of Parliament have to be more committed and involved in order to deal with the great complexities of modern life. This development can, as King argues, have repercussions in government itself, where top politicians, because of their commitment to politics, have less experience of the outside world than their predecessors.

More importantly, politicians are nowadays not only ambitious for office but 'probably also ambitious to express themselves politically – to influence the course of events, to have a say in the formulation of policy, to be in a position effectively to challenge the executive'.[11] Given this new assertiveness, the career politician, King claims, has to channel his or her energies somewhere, and, given that ministerial posts are relatively few in number, this causes the aspiring parliamentarian to turn to other outlets. The new breed therefore become 'good constituency members'; they put a great deal of effort into the new Select Committees; and they demonstrate their independence by refusing always to toe the party line.

George Jones agrees that the trend is for members to immerse themselves either in Select Committees or in local constituency matters, but he argues that it is inappropriate for them to do so. 'MPs seem uncertain of their role. Confused by a babble of conflicting interpretations and envious of foreign models, some have totally misunderstood what they should be doing.'[12] In his view, the main thing that they should be doing is supporting their party either as government or as opposition, and checking the national bureaucracy; backbenchers should neither be debating policy with ministers in Select Committees nor trespassing on the responsibilities of local government. His judgement is simple: 'There are too many MPs, with the result that many MPs have really no satisfying role to perform.'

SKILLS OF THE JOB

Whatever role MPs do find themselves playing, to fulfil the tasks involved in the job, as defined by Hay, 'in a fully acceptable way' requires the deployment of a formidable range of skills and problem-solving techniques. Members 'have to know about party policy and prospects' (including legislation and reaction to it), and how to support or oppose proposals by using procedure in committee work, by participation in debates in the Chamber and party meetings, and by personal contact. They must be adept at persuading the public at large; knowledgeable about the economic and social background and ever-changing interests in their constituencies; sensitive to problems facing constituents and able to take them up with ministers, government departments and agencies, local authorities and councillors; aware of how to secure and, on occasion, avoid publicity. They will probably develop some specialist areas of expertise, and they need a wide (rather than deep) and up-to-date knowledge of current affairs generally. They must have an ability to solve problems 'with breadth and vision and mature judgement'; they should be persuasive and effective lobbyists, and able to plan their time and their goals strategically, though, the consultants concede practically and pragmatically, an adequate MP need not be an 'intellectual giant'.[13] Such a combination of skills seems daunting and, taken at its face value, likely to discourage all but the most confident and talented from even attempting to join the race.

However, some elements of an MP's job are in fact common to a wide and varied range of occupations and professions. Hay seeks to establish comparability with other areas in order to find appropriate salary levels, and MPs might be astonished, or perhaps delighted, to find themselves equated for certain aspects of their jobs (for their 'know-how', problem-solving ability and level of accountability respectively) with, among others, the managing director of a foundry, a director of public relations of a major charity, and the county planner of a large county council.[14]

Perhaps the uniqueness of the job lies in the way it can require and combine differing talents and skills according to the differing demands of time and circumstances. In fact, however, these desirable skills, knowledge and qualities are not prerequisites of the job, and are frequently developed only in the course of performing it. Few new members would claim to have all the skills which Hay outlines. Judgement on how far the ideal has been met, and how successfully talents have been deployed, is passed, somewhat unpredictably, by MPs' paymasters, the electorate. In practice, there clearly exists a wide range of effectiveness and skill amongst MPs of which no one objective or standard measure of success is available, except the highly volatile one of the ballot box.

A FULL-TIME JOB?

Members' jobs are also unusual in the variations in hours worked by different members, and the differing commitments made by MPs to parliamentary and to outside work. Since the TSRB report of 1971, it has been considered that being a member of Parliament is a full-time job, or at least that it should be remunerated as such. 'The job of an MP is increasingly becoming full-time, and progressively more difficult to combine satisfactorily with another regular occupation', said the report.[15] The 1983 TSRB report concurred, adding, however, 'we do not mean by this that members should not be involved in occupations outside the House'. Opinion on how well the country's best interest is served by full-time members has in practice long been divided. Lloyd George stated firmly that 'A member who does his duty to constituents has very little time for anything else', but in the same debate the still-relevant point was made 'that it would be a grave misfortune if the House were to be divorced from the life, the industry, and the commerce of the country by members' withdrawing from other occupations to devote themselves entirely to Parliament.'[16] 'Few would support the idea of a House of Commons composed principally of full-time politicians', said a Select Committee as late as 1954. Full-time members carry with them the risk, it is argued, not only of losing touch with the world they are meant to be representing and helping to govern, but also of compromising their independence, by becoming wholly beholden to their parties. Part-time members, on the other hand, as the TSRB pointed out in 1983, could also have their independence undermined if driven to seek additional employment by financial pressures. Moreover, the jobs compatible with parliamentary life, often at the Bar in London, as company directors, or performing a 'public relations job for a sectional interest'[17] may not necessarily be those most likely 'to enhance the collective understanding of the House in its deliberations on the pressing social, economic and technological problems of the 1980s'.[18] Whatever the nature of the theoretical debate, the Review

Body reported that, of the backbenchers it surveyed, no fewer than 69 per cent reported having regular or occasional paid employment outside Parliament, whether from financial need (despite the best intentions of the earlier TSRB in setting salary levels specifically to obviate such a need), or for other reasons.[19] The TSRB further found in its 1983 survey that, on top of their work in Parliament, over a third of members with outside commitments spent up to five hours a week on them, some 7 per cent more than 20 hours and the majority somewhere between the two.[20] The mean of time spent on outside occupations overall was ten hours a week.

MPS' WORKING HOURS

Whether they have outside occupations or not, nearly all back-benchers are in practice full-time Members of Parliament. 94 per cent of them reported devoting an average of at least 40 hours a week, over the year, to their parliamentary duties. 96 per cent considerably exceeded the standard industrial working week in the session, and 44 per cent did so even in the recess. The average working week over the year was found to be 62 hours, 69 when the House was sitting, and 42 in the recess. Averages do, of course disguise extremes, and, while seven of the TSRB's sample claimed to work 101 hours or more a week on parliamentary business, five candidly claimed to work an average of between 26 and 30 hours a week over the year as a whole, while three admitted to between only six and ten hours a week in the recess.[21]

Although some members may restrict their parliamentary work-load and put in comparatively few hours, the opportunities abound for workaholics to indulge themselves, both in the constituency and at Westminster. Members divide their time between constituency and Westminster in differing proportions. Over the year as a whole, taking the mean, the TSRB found that members spent over twice as long at Westminster as in the constituency, with the proportion of time in the House rising to over two thirds during the session. In the recesses, members tended to spend three quarters of their time in the constituency or on parliamentary business away from the House, perhaps abroad. When the House is sitting, members spend, typically, four days a week at Westminster and at least one in the constituency.

THE PARLIAMENTARY YEAR AND THE PARLIAMENTARY DAY

Taking the job in Westminster alone, British MPs are hard-working by international standards. The British Parliament meets on more days, and for longer hours, than any other Parliament in the world. In recent decades sessions have averaged some 34 weeks a year, with length of sitting days averaging 8¾ hours. The parliamentary year opens with the Queen's Speech in November. There are then recesses of between two and three weeks in late December and early January, about a week at Easter, and a week or so for the Spring Bank Holiday at the end of May. The long summer recess lasts from about late July until mid-October (roughly 11 weeks), when the House meets to finish business, as necessary, before prorogation. Uncertainty about the precise dates of the Parliamentary year is a constant source of irritation to members, who deem it unnecessary, though it is an inconvenience shared with many other Parliaments around the world.

From Monday to Thursday, the House sits from 2.30 p.m., after Prayers, to 10.30 p.m., the 'appointed time' on 'normal' nights, after a half-hour adjournment debate on a matter raised by a member and answered by a minister. On Friday, it meets at 9.30 a.m. and rises at 3 p.m. or earlier. In recent sessions, however, the House has regularly sat after 10.30 p.m. on as many as 8 out of 10 sitting days. The averages for the length of the daily sittings include Fridays, when the House often rises early, thus disguising the extent to which many sittings go on late into the night. As many as half have extended beyond midnight, which means that on average members may be going home after midnight every other night, and in practice, on several nights in a row.[22] Such hours are the bane of members' lives, the source of their greatest complaint about Parliament. They are only made bearable for the conscientious member by the possibility of arranging, with the agreement of the whips, to 'pair' with an opposition member so that both have an occasional night off without threatening the government majority or the opposition's credibility, or by the occasional *bisque*, a system which allows government MPs one night out each week, determined by a letter of the alphabet.

Marathon sittings on issues of importance – for example, the 32-hour, 13-minute sitting on the Local Government (Interim Provisions) Bill in 1983–4, which abolished the Greater London Council and metropolitan counties – or the regular and predictable all-night sessions when members raise a series of subjects for debate on the Consolidated Fund Bill, are not the real problem. Rather, it is the uncertainty and unpredictability of late-night sittings, and their cumulative effect in reducing the bright-eyed activists of the new session in November to the sometimes noticeably weary and crumpled legislators released to the restorative of the summer recess. 'A crucial issue in Parliament is how to stop late sittings', said one member, speaking for many; 'they are the worst feature of my life.'

It is not surprising to find that considerable support for reform is voiced by members. However, an experiment with morning sittings was tried and abandoned in 1967. Members' doubts about this change stemmed not from sheer masochism, but more probably from a lively appreciation, even amongst those without outside interests which they pursued before lunch of how many demands there already were on their mornings. Many feared that, if introduced permanently, morning sittings might not reduce the incidence of late-night sittings but simply furnish extra time for government business. Thus members would increasingly be caught at both the beginning and the end of the day.

The length of time the House sits is, however, only one indicator of the hours members work at Westminster. Many MPs will have started their day there long before business begins in the Chamber. Equally, some, confident of the time of the evening's division, will have slipped away to attend to parliamentary or non-parliamentary business outside the House, or to relax at a social event, to return only as the division bells ring. Not many will stay in the Chamber all the time in the evening, even if they are in the House. In one week in January 1984, for example, observers claim to have recorded that, on successive nights, 42 members were in the Chamber before a division in which 494 votes were counted, 30 before one in which 298 voted, 121 before one in which 381 voted, and, even for an important debate where a backbench rebellion occurred, only 234 MPs were in the Chamber though 535 voted in the division.[23]

HOURS IN THE CHAMBER

It is, of course, a popular misconception to view the Chamber as

the main focus of an MP's work at Westminster, and to take a
sparsely populated Chamber as a reflection of how much, or little,
work members are doing. Any long-term effect on attendance in
the Chamber of televising proceedings remains to be seen, but in
1983 it was estimated that members spent between twelve and
fifteen hours a week in the Chamber, participating in the legislative
process, listening, speaking (or waiting to speak) in debates, taking
part in Question Time, and influencing affairs as best they could as
private members. This could be by raising topics in adjournment
debates, focusing attention on particular issues through private
members' motions or ten-minute-rule Bills, and, occasionally – but
only with government support, luck and good management –
getting a private member's Bill through the Commons and *en route*
to the Statute Book. Backbench members do not have much
opportunity to determine what subjects will be debated in the
Chamber, and they must ballot for the limited time available to
them to bring in a Bill or move a motion of their own devising.
Apart from this, almost the only opportunity they have to instigate
debate is through ten-minute-rule Bills, which can be introduced
on a first-come, first-served basis with a ten-minute speech after
Question Time on Tuesdays and Wednesdays.

The figures for the 1983–4 session illustrate the limitations on
private members' time. It was a hard-working session, with
members sitting for 213 days (a figure exceeded only once in the
previous ten years, in the 1979–80 session), and marching through
the division lobbies 482 times (a process which took, incidentally,
an estimated 93 hours and 23 minutes). Private members selected
the topics under consideration for 19 per cent of the time, made up
of 3 per cent on Bills, 5 per cent on motions and 11 per cent on
business such as the half-hour adjournments before the close of
business, holiday adjournments and topics debated under the
Consolidated Fund Bills. The range of interests and enthusiasms
demonstrated was wide. Bills introduced included the Chronically
Sick and Disabled Persons Amendment Bill (which only got a first
reading) and the Immigration Offences (Amendment) Bill (which
got to the second-reading stage). Private members' motions included 'The Plight of the Younger Generation' and 'The Encourage-
ment of Human Organ Donorship'. A total of 555 hours, or 29 per
cent of the House's time, was spent on the stages of government
Bills which became law, such as the Data Protection Bill, the Rates
Bill, and the London Regional Transport Bill, with most time spent

debating the general principles in the Bills, on second readings, or in more detailed discussion in the Committee of the whole House. Delegated legislation (discussion of statutory instruments) took 9 per cent of the time, European Community business 3 per cent, and other government motions 15 per cent. The remaining quarter of the House's time was spent on questions, private Bills (introduced by petition, usually by public authorities but sometimes by private companies and individuals, to enable them to acquire additional legal powers; examples are the Ginns and Gutteridge Leicester (Crematorium) Bill and the Associated British Ports Bill), and debates on matters raised by the opposition, ranging from 'The Deterioration of the Transport System', to 'The Deployment of Cruise Missiles', and 'The Future of the Shipbuilding Industry'. During the session, 13 out of the 18 private members' Bills that were introduced became law, since they were either entirely uncontroversial or had government support, compared to 75 government bills. In the ten years between 1978 and 1988 some 14 per cent of Private Members' Bills received the Royal Assent, compared with 95 per cent of government Bills.[24] Such statistics reflect the limitations of the role of 'legislator' for private members, and illustrate why, in their more pessimistic moments, they can feel themselves to be little more than 'lobby fodder' in the House. Defeat of government legislation backed by a 3-line whip, on Second Reading, like that of the Shops Bill in 1986, is rare; loyalty, party discipline and personal ambition for office serve to discourage an independent stance in the Divisions.

New members tend to spend longer in the Chamber than their established colleagues. Ann Clwyd, for example, reckoned in her first Parliament to spend four or five hours a day in the Chamber, because 'I see it as part of my education', and Archy Kirkwood saw Question Time in particular as 'one way of learning the business'. Many who start in this way, however, find that, as their obligations multiply, they are forced to become more selective in their priorities, and time in the Chamber suffers. This was Mark Fisher's experience. In his first year he spoke sixteen times and attended most Question Times, but in his second year the need to respond to other pressures had the effect of cutting his attendance at Question Time to occasions when questions relating to his special interests, Treasury and education matters, were raised, or when he himself had questions down, and he spoke only five or six times in debate.

The growth of committee and constituency work have been major factors affecting the time members are willing or able to spend in the Chamber. Members do cite other reasons, such as feelings that 'the debate never changes anyone's mind', that debates are becoming increasingly specialised and detailed, that too many speeches are 'long and boring' and, in short, that proceedings are ritualised and so dominated by Ministers and frontbenchers as to be deeply frustrating to backbenchers. 'Members', as the TSRB says, 'tend to go into the Chamber to speak rather than to listen.' As Julian Critchley put it, 'It is a strain to sit in the Chamber with no certainty of being called upon to speak (unlike the Lords) from 3.30 to, say, 8.15, listening to the contributions of your colleagues, helpless to prevent the theft of your better arguments, watching the number of MPs present dwindle to half a dozen seated on either side when you are called.'[25] The uncertainty of being called is a real deterrent to attendance; where the party in government has a big majority, its backbenchers are so numerous that they have little chance of speaking, and opposition backbench spokesmen are also unlikely to be called except on their specialism. According to Mr Speaker Weatherill, 'if the Speaker is entirely fair, the average member will be called four times a year ... most of his constituents think he should be called four times a week, and he thinks he should be called eight times a week. But it doesn't work like that.' He did maintain, however, that it is possible for backbenchers to swing a debate by force of their argument, and reported that he had heard 19 such speeches in the 1983–7 Parliament, and four in the first year of the 1987–8 Parliament. A few members claim quite frankly that they are reluctant to go into the Chamber in a poorly attended debate, precisely because the whips are likely to press them to contribute to it, whether they want to or not. Most, however, seem to identify with Tony Banks' sentiments, if not his turn of phrase in the debate of 14 July 1988, 'Nothing is more frustrating than sitting here either like a Cicero or a Demosthenes, burning to speak, while some old bore goes on for hours and hours rambling endlessly on.' It was expected that the televising of proceedings would increase the numbers of members anxious to speak and to be seen doing so. The new rule of July 1988, giving the Speaker power to limit backbench contributions to ten minutes within a two hour slot in major debates did not remove the privilege of frontbenchers, or the uncertainty as to who would be called, but it was welcomed as a means of perhaps doubling the number of backbenchers able to speak.

The exodus of members at the end of Question Time bears witness to its comparative popularity. It takes place each afternoon from Monday to Thursday and lasts nearly an hour, with each departmental minister taking a turn on a rota basis about once every four weeks, and the Prime Minister answering for fifteen minutes on Tuesdays and Thursdays. Question Time may be more entertaining, and on occasion more dramatic, than many other parliamentary occasions, and is a means of having useful information put on the record. However, its value as a method of scrutinising or embarrassing the government is increasingly called into question. In the 1983–4 session, the answers to over 56,000 questions were recorded in Hansard, but only some 9400 of them were answered orally, including the potentially awkward 'supplementaries', of which ministers have no notice and which are traditionally one of the highlights of the democratic process. In fact, though some 70 or 80 Questions are tabled to major Departments on an average day, only the first 15 to 20 on the Order Paper are answered orally. Their position on the Order Paper will have been decided by ballot ten sitting days earlier in the 'four o'clock shuffle' performed by the Clerks. Opposition members, in particular, can feel that the odds are weighted too much against the private member at Question Time and that Ministers can nowadays find it all too easy to avoid a real grilling. Others are critical of the use made of Question Time by some of their colleagues: 'an excuse for yah-boo politics', one called it, remarking that he for one shunned it.

Prime Minister's Question Time at 3.15 p.m. on Tuesdays and Thursdays is the Chamber's major crowd-puller, among strangers and members alike, but it too is much criticised: for example, as 'pure cabaret', a 'farce', and an 'exercise of no real value, creating a poor public image of the House'. Only four or five Questions can be answered in the fifteen minutes allowed, with priority for the frontbench and Privy Councillors. On average, a backbencher gets 'one chance every 12 months', according to Clare Short,[28] though the assiduous who put their questions on a regular basis may be called perhaps twice as often.

In the familiar pattern, there is a wide variation amongst members in the use they make of Question Time. Austin Mitchell has shown how in the 1979–80 session some members made considerably greater use of their opportunities than others did. For example, while Bob Cryer, Labour member for Keighley, asked 605 oral and written questions, and Albert McQuarrie, Conservative member for Aberdeenshire East, asked 511, Gordon Bagier, Labour member for Sunderland South, and Julian Amery, then Conservative member for Brighton Pavilion, asked only 13 questions each.[29]

Indeed, an analysis of the work of the Chamber as a whole over six days in March and April 1988 found that 124 backbenchers (88 Conservatives, 28 Labour and 3 SLD) neither spoke nor tabled any written questions during that period. This compared with the record of such 'workhorses' as Tony Banks, who made three speeches, asked 14 oral questions, tabled written questions and voted in every whipped Division, and Bob Cryer, with his four speeches, seven written questions and eight oral interventions.[30]

COMMITTEES

The same degree of variation exists between members in the extent to which they serve on committees, whose burgeoning in recent years has been an important factor in changing the shape of life at Westminster. It is not, of course, mandatory for members to serve either on the Standing Committees, which consider Bills clause by clause and delegated legislation, nor on the Select Committees, which consider particular subjects or the affairs of government departments. There is, however, a strong expectation that members will serve when asked to do so, and newer members are often given the less popular committees, to learn the job and develop expertise, which is important to the future of the House as well as to that of the individual member.

The expectation is not always fulfilled. Richard Crossman recorded in his diaries that he, for one, attended a Standing Committee for the first time after thirteen years in Parliament.

In the first year of the 1987 Parliament, about 10 per cent of members did not serve on any Select or Standing Committee. The patterns of attendance can vary widely, as a study of 1984–5 demonstrates. 11 MPs attended more than 50 Select Committee meetings, but 442 attended fewer than ten; 95 MPs attended more than 30 Standing Committee meetings, and 403 fewer than ten.[32] Scottish MPs work particularly hard in committees because of their special responsibilities for Scottish legislation, and they tend to be near the top in the league table of attendances at committee meetings.

Standing Committees comprise some 16–20 members, appointed by the Committee of Selection guided by the whips. Scottish Standing Committees consider Scottish legislation, and the Scottish and Welsh Grand Committees, and the Northern Ireland Committee, debate Scottish, Welsh, and Irish affairs respectively; each of the others, lettered A, B, C, and so on (in busy sessions reaching K), work on the details of a Bill allotted to them for consideration, with sometimes as many as twenty sessions on each. Such committees meet at least twice a week, on Tuesday, Wednesday and Thursday mornings, from 10.30 a.m. to 1 p.m., and at other times as necessary, sometimes sitting throughout the night. The composition of committees reflects the proportions of the parties in the House. Individual members may secure amendments to government bills in committee, but usually only with the support of a minister, an overwhelmingly good case, or luck and sleight of hand.

The longer-established Select Committees include the important Public Accounts Committee, the Committees on Privileges, on Procedure, on Consolidation Bills, on House of Commons Services (with four sub-committees), on Liaison, on Members' Interests, on Sound Broadcasting, on Statutory Instruments and on European Legislation, and the Committee of the Parliamentary Commissioner for Administration. The departmental Select Committees, which were set up in 1979 in response to all-party pressure and grew out of the earlier experimental 'Crossman' Select Committees, have added considerably to the workload of the average backbencher. They comprise some 9–13 members each, and have the task of examining 'the expenditure, administration and policy of ... principal Government Departments ... and associated public bodies'. Each committee 'shadows' a government department. The fourteen departmental Select Committees currently functioning are those concerned with Agriculture; Defence; Education, Science and the Arts; Employment; Energy; the Environment; Foreign Affairs; Home Affairs; Industry and Trade; Scottish Affairs; Social Services; Transport; the Treasury and Civil Service; and Welsh Affairs. The committees have no executive power, only the right to scrutinise and criticise policy. However, their hearings and reports and the publicity attending them can influence public opinion and thus policy-making, and, compared to the ritualised Question Time or set-piece debate, they provide a highly effective forum in which to press a minister and his officials. This is perhaps the main reason why they are popular with members who serve on them (nearly a quarter of the membership of the House) and why the attendance rate has been uniformly high, averaging about 75 per cent, despite the heavy demands such committees can make on members' time.

They meet at least once a week and bear a heavy workload, often involving even more than other committees, a considerable amount of travel both to other parts of Britain and abroad, and a great deal of preparatory work, reading the evidence submitted to committees, consulting with interested parties, planning suitable lines of investigation, and devising and putting questions to witnesses. For example, in the three sessions between 1979 and 1983, the Agriculture Committee met for a total of 59 evidence-taking sessions and 40 deliberative sessions; the Defence Committee made a total of 16 visits in the United Kingdom and 10 abroad, while the Education Committee made 41 in the UK and 7 abroad; members on the Trade and Industry Select Committees had no fewer than 172 departmental memoranda to absorb, and those on Transport a less demanding 53. As one member commented, 'there is at least six inches [of paper] to read a week'. The Foreign Affairs Select Committee and the Treasury and Civil Service Select Committee (with their sub-committees) examined officials from government departments on 201 and 238 occasions, and ministers on 27 and 21 occasions, respectively, as well as other witnesses, such as academics, businessmen, and representatives of the CBI and TUC. Together, the committees published a huge quantity of material, over 200 reports and a wealth of evidence.[33] It is not altogether surprising, therefore, to find that, though the consensus amongst the MPs polled by the All-Party Reform Group is that the main role of Select Committees should be in scrutinising the administration, most believe in fact that they have been most successful as a means of informing the House and contributing to the debate on current issues. At the same time there is an increasing demand among would-be reformers like Graham Allen MP, that their impact be enhanced by having at least one report from each Select Committee debated on the floor of the House.

Members agree that committees of all sorts are among the most time-consuming part of being an MP at Westminster, especially if they take a leading role on them. They can spend up to 50 per cent of their time in the House on Committee business. There are an average of eight committees working every Tuesday, Wednesday and Thursday morning and four in the afternoons. In the 1983 Parliament, Michael Hirst MP reported being in committee three mornings a week, and also on the Scottish Grand Committee, meeting from time to time in Edinburgh; Angela Rumbold MP, as a backbencher, spent some 20 hours a week in committee, a high but not unusual amount of time; Tom Sackville MP reckoned to spend two hours a week on the All Party Committee on Drug Abuse, and some 10–15 hours a week on the Finance Bill, while Roger Freeman MP found that the Treasury Select Committee and the Finance Bill took up some 15–20 hours a week. It can be hard work in committee, and not merely long hours. The work is often detailed and demanding of members' expertise.

Committee work, as Tom Sackville's schedule suggests, need not be confined to the official parliamentary and legislative committees. There are a plethora of all-party and party groups in the House, covering a wide spectrum of interests and topics relevant, and indeed integral, to members' constituency, personal and political interests. The all-party groups are multifarious, waxing and waning with the topicality of the subject, and the enthusiasms of current members. In 1988, there were about 100 such groups, excluding those concerned with social, sports and religious activities, demanding the attention of some 250 MPs as officers, and many more as ordinary members, meeting at varying intervals, some frequently, and some quite rarely. Such groups are as various as the Animal Welfare Parliamentary Group, the Boys' Brigade Group, the Campaign for the Homeless and Rootless, the Esperanto Parliamentary Group, the Death Grant Lobby, the Industrial Common Ownership Movement, the Knitting and Hosiery Industries Group, the Roads Study Group, the Scotch Whisky Group, and the World Government Parliamentary Group. They are complemented by the numerous all-party country groups, centred on one country, such as the Afghan Parliamentary Group, the Belize Parliamentary Group, the Madagascar Parliamentary Group and the Singapore Parliamentary Group, all organised under the auspices of the Commonwealth Parliamentary Association or the Inter-Parliamentary Union. These groups include in their membership the overwhelming majority of members. In 1988 there were over 100 all-party country groups, each with between two and six

MPs acting as officers. The country groups are a useful way for members to develop mutually beneficial first-hand contacts with foreign embassies in London, as well as with sources in the countries themselves. Similarly, the subject groups, through their associations with particular industries or other areas of interest, can be very useful both in increasing MPs' sources of information and in broadening their perspective. The level of activity of both subject and country groups, and the attendance rate of members, vary enormously, but active involvement with them can be very time-consuming, including as it may dealing with representations from the special-interest groups associated with a particular country, seeking information from the government and Whitehall and attending social functions. They are, however, an important part of the political, and indeed the legislative, process, useful to governments in keeping them informed of feeling in the House on different issues, and often themselves having an influence on the government's policy and legislation.[34]

It is not surprising to find that party affairs can make considerable demands on members' time at Westminster. Each of the major parties has a weekly meeting, lasting routinely between an hour and an hour and a half. There are, in addition, the various faction or 'ginger' groups within the parties, such as the Solidarity and Tribune groups in the Labour Party, and the Conservative Party's Monday Club and Tory Reform Group. There are numerous party subject committees, as well as the regional committees, which bring together members from particular areas of the country. At the last count, there were some 23 subject committees and 7 regional groups in the Conservative Party, and 19 and 9 respectively in the Labour Party.[35] Party subject groups usually feature larger in the lives of opposition members, for whom they are a means of influencing and developing party policy, than in the lives of government backbenchers. Meetings of all these groups take place on a regular basis, often weekly, and in the early evening. They may be poorly attended, but a topical issue or particular speakers can draw a large attendance, and members differ, as always, in how important they think it is to attend them. Committees settling the future of the Alliance parties were clearly time-consuming for the members concerned after the 1987 election. In the 1983 Parliament both Dennis Canavan (Labour) and George Walden (Conservative) reckoned to spend some two hours a week on their different party committees, while Angela Rumbold (Conservative) as a backbencher estimated the time she spent there at about three or four hours and Ann Clwyd (Labour) at six or seven. Whatever the individual's commitment, the cumulative effect of proliferating party committees has been to encourage the trend for the focus of members' activity to be elsewhere than on the floor of the House.

CONSTITUENCY WORKLOAD

Dealing with an increasing workload from the constituency, particularly of the welfare-officer/social-work variety, has been an important part of the member's job over the last twenty years or so. It is a feature of the MP's work at Westminster, as well as in the constituency, for some problems which come to light in constituency surgeries cannot be dealt with on the spot and need detailed follow-up in London. Such problems, together with circulars from pressure groups and constituents' unsolicited views on current events, form part of the considerable weight of correspondence all members receive daily. Peter Bruinvels MP has estimated that members together received some 6.5 million postal items in 1984, an average of 14,500 letters daily through the House of Commons sorting-office, or some 115 per member a week. Most MPs claim to spend at least two hours a day dealing with correspondence, though skilled, experienced and resourceful secretaries can reduce the burden for them enormously.

The size of a member's postbag, and the mix – how much from pressure groups and how much from constituents, say – varies greatly according to the member and the nature of the constituency. A survey carried out by the Letter Writing Bureau and based on questionnaires completed by 196 MPs (with results reported in *The Times* on 7 July 1986), put the average number of letters received by members slightly higher than the 1984 figure, at 33 a day. It found that members from the south-west received most mail, with 42 letters each, while those from Northern Ireland received only 21 a day. Housing and social security were the most common constituency matters raised, followed by education, with unemployment and taxes lower down the list. The most contentious topical issues then were the teachers' dispute and Sunday trading, while embryo experiments, abortion and animal welfare recur as perennials. Campaigns by pressure groups on controversial issues such as these do swell postbags enormously, and seem to be on the increase.

Of members we spoke to, Roger Freeman calculated that about half the mail he received was concerned with constituency matters and half with finance, his specialisation, while Archy Kirkwood divided his up into about a third constituency, a third pressure groups and a third on subjects with which he dealt as Alliance spokesman. George Walden found that his mail was chiefly from constituents, but was not particularly heavy, as it took him only about six hours a week to deal with it. 'Mine is not a socio-economically deprived constituency', he explains, although this can be just the kind which generates mail, from constituents who may be more leisured, literate and opinionated. As if to confirm this point, Ann Clwyd reckons to have only about twelve letters a week from constituents, because, as she says, 'people in my kind of constituency don't write, they come to surgeries'. Alan Amos, with mainly rural constituents, was 'amazed at how the flow of correspondence never lets up' and attributes this partly to the spread of desktop computers. Graham Allen, a fifty-letters-a-day man was, on the other hand, surprised not to get even more. Though writing the replies was time-consuming, he felt it was important for a new member, particularly, to get the feel of the case load. Many agree with him, and like Gillian Shephard will want to see all the letters even though routine responses may be entrusted to a secretary. Methods of dealing with mail vary enormously too. Stuart Bell has about 180 letters a week and redirects them to the constituency, where his wife handles them. He saves the compli-cated cases to deal with in the quiet evening hours at Westminster between 5 and 9 p.m. Bryan Gould adopts a brisk and business-like approach, and with the help of two computers and his wife, acting as secretary, is often, he says, able to deal with his 80 or so letters a day in less than an hour.

Some constituency problems will require considerable follow-up. They may involve individual cases of hardship or injustice, or the economic or environmental well-being of the constituency as a whole. Members may forward letters, or themselves write, to the ministers responsible in the relevant government departments, asking for clarifications and explanations, giving opinions and making protests. House of Commons notepaper, it has been remarked, is one of members' most important weapons. Their correspondence will get special treatment from departments, in most cases by-passing the lower levels of the bureaucracy, and avoiding the stock answer, even if they do not achieve a change in decisions on individual cases. Members may occasionally meet with departmental officials, but usually they deal with the ministers if they want to press a case, either meeting them formally, or catching them in the corridor for a quiet word. They may raise an issue by asking a question in the House, though the more cynical would say that, if they want to get their name in the papers, members ask a question; if they want something done, they contact the minister, and, indeed, often more can be achieved informally, by quiet diplomacy, than in the public forum. If still not satisfied, however, a member may 'go public', seeking an adjournment debate on a particular topic and forcing the minister publicly to justify his decision and his department's course of action. This also gives the member the opportunity to set out the arguments on his or her side for everyone, including constituents, to hear. Causes of general concern to the constituency, rather than individual hardship cases, tend to be those which are dealt with publicly in questions and adjournment debates. In one month in July 1988, subjects brought up on the motion for adjournment, at the end of the day's business, included problems of the footwear and textile industries in Leicester, the demands on the Search and Rescue Services in S. W. England, the special needs of education in Rochdale and of Maternity Services in Bexley, and the circumstances of the Barn Elms Reservoir in Richmond and Barnes.

Seeing constituents can be time-consuming, too. Members with constituencies close to London may well find there is something of a trade-off between the time their colleagues spend in travelling to far-flung constituencies and the time they have to spend meeting constituents, showing school parties round, entertaining women's groups to stawberries and cream on the terrace, or local businessmen to lunch or dinner. Members have different attitudes on what can be regarded here as a chore or a pleasure. Some try to limit the number of people they see at the House, and prefer not to spend time showing them round the Palace, whereas others tend to feel that this is part of the job. Other activities on behalf of the constituency and constituents may involve interviews with the media to explain, or campaign on, constituency issues; consultations with members and interest groups from neighbouring constituencies; or simply trying to obtain tickets for the Stranger's Gallery for Question Time. Most members find it hard, as well as impolitic, to avoid seeing the constituents who drop into the House unannounced.

Filling out and setting off the major pieces in the kaleidoscopic pattern that makes up a member's life at Westminster are the fragments, from composing amendments, tabling early-day motions and gathering support for them, to managing the work of secretaries and research assistants which, together and over a period, can be time-consuming and energy-sapping. Much of what members do depends on the acquisition, absorption and understanding of information, whether this comes via the postbag, through the press and television, Parliamentary Papers, *Hansard*, seminars, government briefings, research, or even through discussion or gossip with colleagues in the Tea Room, the Smoking-Room or the bars. Dealing with the attentions of lobbyists and pressure groups and their material, whether for local or national causes, is an increasing burden. Most hard-working members agree that the opportunities for quiet reflection and research in their own rooms or in the Library are scarce indeed, unless they are determined to make space for them in busy schedules. Social events, state functions such as addresses to members of both Houses by visiting foreign dignitaries, 'off the record' conversations with lobby correspondents, interviews with radio and television and other journalists, sessions with earnest researchers and the completing of survey forms – all these can be a part of the job at Westminster. They can help leaven, from time to time, the solid, grinding, hard work of committees, the disappointments and frustrations of the Chamber, and the long hours of boredom during late-night sittings, when, too tired to work, members wait for that last division bell and the freedom to go home.

NOTES

1. *Review Body on Top Salaries: Report no. 20. review of Parliamentary Pay and Allowances*, Cmnd 8881 (HMSO, 1983) 'The Pay of Members of Parliament and Ministers of the Crown', vols I and II, and *Report no. 24, Review of Parliamentary Allowances*, vols I and II, Cmnd 131 – I and II (HMSO, 1987).
2. A. Mitchell, *Westminster Man: A Tribal Anthology of the Commons People* (Methuen, 1982) p. 60.
3. *HC Deb.*, 82, col. 1452, 12 July 1985.

4. Discussed by Hay in *Review Body on Top Salaries: Report no. 20*, II 149–53.
5. Ibid., pp. 149–50.
6. P. Norton, 'Dear Minister.... The Importance of MP to Minister Correspondence', *Parliamentary Affairs*, 35 no. 1 (1982) 66.
7. D. Searing, 'The Role of the Good Constituency Member and the Practice of Representation in Great Britain', *Journal of Politics*, 47 (1985) 355.
8. Ibid., p. 371.
9. Ibid., p. 379
10. A. King, 'The Rise of the Career Politician in Britain – and its Consequences', *British Journal of Political Science*, II, pt iii (1981) 249–85.
11. Ibid., p. 279.
12. G. W. Jones, 'The House of Commons: A Threat to Good Government?', *London Review of Public Administration*, 16 (1984) 22–5.
13. *Review Body on Top Salaries: Report no. 20*, II, 156.
14. Ibid., pp. 194–202.
15. *Review Body on Top Salaries: First Report, Ministers of the Crown and Members of Parliament*, Cmnd 4836 (HMSO, 1971) p. 4; quoted in D. Judge, 'The Politics of MPs' Pay', *Parliamentary Affairs*, 37, no. 1 (1984) 8.
16. *HC Deb.*, 29, cols 1383 ff., 10 Aug 1911.
17. Frederick Willey, *The Honourable Member* (Sheldon, 1974) p. 66; quoted by Judge, in *Parliamentary Affairs*, 37, no. 1, p. 60.
18. Judge, ibid.
19. *Review Body on Top Salaries: Report no. 20*, table 6, p. 14.
20. Ibid., table 7, p. 15.
21. Ibid., tables 3 and 4, pp. 12–13.
22. R. Evans, 'MPs Forced into More Post-Midnight Sittings', *The Times*, 25 Feb 1985, pp. 1 and 28.
23. *Mail on Sunday*, 29 Feb 1984, p. 11.
24. See *HC Deb.*, 78, cols 127–9, 1 May 1985; and *House of Commons Sessional Information Digest, 1983–84* (compiled by the Public Information Office, Department of the Library, Dec 1984); D. Marsh and M. Read, *Private Members' Bills* (Cambridge University Press, 1988); *HC Deb.*, 134 c 715w, 10 June 1988.
25. J. Critchley, *Westminster Blues: Minor Chords* (Elm Tree Books/Hamish Hamilton, 1985) p. 118.
26. *Weekend World* on London Weekend Television, 8 May, 1988.
27. See House of Commons Information Office Factsheet no. 4, *Questions* (Dec 1987).
28. Clare Short, 'Frustrations of life on the back benches', *New Statesman*, 27 April 1988.
29. Mitchell, *Westminster Man*, pp. 137–9.
30. Anthony Bevins, 'Backbench MPs face daily frustration', *Independent*, 16 May 1988.
31. *The Backbench Diaries of Richard Crossman*, ed. J. Morgan (Hamish Hamilton/Cape, 1981) p. 734.
32. See the *Guardian*, 31 May 1986.

33. D. Englefield (ed.), *Commons Select Committees: Catalysts for Progress?* (Longman, 1984); and G. Drewry, *The New Select Committees: A Study of the 1979 Reforms* (Oxford University Press, 1985).

34. See House of Commons Information Office Factsheets no. 7 *All Party Subject Groups in the House of Commons* (rev. edn, May 1982), and no. 8 *All Party Country Groups* (rev. edn, Feb 1982).

35. P. Norton, 'Party Organisation in the House of Commons', *Parliamentary Affairs*, 31, no. 4 (1978).

4

A Parliamentary Day

*To do the job ... requires a par-
ticularly thick-skinned workaholic.*
(Austin Mitchell MP)

What do hard-working and conscientious MPs do all day at the Palace of Westminster? What role do they play as backbenchers? If the job of a member of Parliament is to legislate, to keep a check on the executive, and to represent his or her constituents, how is all this done?

It is axiomatic that the government of the day sees getting its own legislation through Parliament as its main priority, and therefore wants as little opposition to this as possible. Government backbenchers naturally recognise this aim and indeed approve of it, but, because they themselves are not ministers (there are only about a hundred members of the government), they see their role as one not merely of assisting the passage of legislation, but also of scrutinising executive action, as well as attempting to influence their own party and acting for their constituents. Select Committees are one important way of checking the executive, while party meetings and party subject committees provide opportunities for backbenchers to influence the leadership.

Opposition backbenchers, with only the very tenuous power of delay, see their role differently. They can sometimes either stop legislation going through altogether (but only in a hung parliament) or amend it in a way that is more satisfactory to them. At the same time, they too, but with perhaps greater determination, scrutinise the activities of the government of the day. Like their opposite numbers, they also act for their constituents and attempt to influence their own party over various policy issues.

Let us follow two hypothetical backbenchers, a government and an opposition member, through a day at Westminster and see how they carry out their respective roles.

Mr Able, who is a government backbencher, comes into the House most mornings either to deal with his mail or to sit on the Standing Committee of which he is a member. Mr Able wants to get on; he is a new member and has agreed to serve on the Committee to demonstrate to the whips (the administrators of the party) that he is a reliable, hard-working sort of person whom they ought to look upon with favour.

He may be involved in the Chamber in passing legislation at any or all of the five stages to the passage of a Bill. The first is when the Bill (the contents of which have previously been discussed in detail by ministers and their civil servants in the relevant department) is presented to the House of Commons. This first reading is a mere formality: the House of Commons is simply informed that a Bill entitled, say, 'Dogs – Fouling of Public Areas Bill', is being put to the House and will be printed that same day. There is no discussion of the Bill at this stage.

The next stage, the second reading, is when debate on a Bill begins. Usually some time elapses between the first and second readings, as the Bill has to take its turn with the rest of the government's legislation. Notice of the debate is short, being given the Thursday before the week in which it will be held.

During the second reading, the principle of the Bill is discussed, but not particular clauses. The debate is formally opened, after Question Time, by a minister in charge. The opposition spokesman who is 'shadowing' the minister will reply on behalf of the opposition, after which all interested members from both sides of the House will hope to catch the Speaker's eye and be called to speak. The debate is finally closed by the frontbencher deputed to wind up for the opposition and by another government minister. The vote is then taken. Bells ring all over the Palace of Westminster, in outlying offices, and even in some nearby restaurants. Members of the government leave the Chamber by a door behind the Speaker's Chair, and in this case move left into the Aye lobby to support the Bill; members opposing the measure go out through the door facing the Speaker's Chair behind the Bar, and they turn left into the No lobby to register dissent. All names are then publicly recorded in the appropriate Aye or No column by clerks who tick off the MPs' names from an alphabetical list. Two tellers from each lobby then report back to the Speaker in the Chamber.

Assuming that the government has won the vote on the second reading, the Bill then moves on to the third stage, called the committee stage. Having had its first generalised airing on the floor of the House, the Bill is now scrutinised clause by clause either in the Chamber by the Committee of the whole House (usually because it is of constitutional importance or too important to give to Standing Committees), or, more often, by a small Standing Committee. This normally meets twice a week from 10.30 a.m. to 1 p.m. and its composition reflects the distribution of the political parties in the House.

As soon as all the clauses, plus any amendments, have been debated and approved, the Bill is ready for the fourth stage in its passage. This is the report stage, when the House is presented with a version of the Bill which has evolved out of the deliberations of the Standing Committee. Further and final amendments can be discussed only on the basis of this new version.

Once the debate on the report stage is over, the Bill moves to the third reading, the fifth and final stage of its passage through the Commons. Discussion of the Bill is now based on the final profile to come out of the report stage. The third reading, like the first, is seen as a mere formality, though there can be debate.

Once the Bill has passed its third reading, it goes to the House of Lords. Any change made there, chiefly at the committee stage, has to be agreed by the Commons before the Bill receives the Royal Assent and becomes law.

Let us now return to Mr Able and his parliamentary day. On the morning in question he strides along the Committee Corridor to take his place among the government members appointed to his particular Standing Committee. He knows that his role is primarily to vote in support of the government and that he will be encouraged neither to speak (which would hold up proceedings) nor to suggest amendments (which would change the nature of the Bill, and earn him grave government displeasure). He is there simply to vote at the right time. He has already got a measure of the clause that the Committee is debating, and knows that, as the opposition is in full tongue, that particular clause will not be voted on for some time. So he goes in armed with background papers he wants to read, and the notes for a difficult speech he has to make in his constituency at the weekend. His powers of concentration being excellent, this morning, so far as he is concerned, will not be entirely wasted. He also has time to make a few telephone calls in the corridor outside the committee room. His speech begins to shape up and he decides to begin work on another one, which he intends to give that very evening on the second reading of a Bill extending the power of local authorities to deal with footpaths and bridleways, in which he has a particular interest. Opposition backbenchers, he has noted in passing, have been in great form, hammering away at the government's proposed legislation. They at least, he thinks sadly, have been allowed to speak. In the end, of course, the government majority is such that most of the clauses debated that day are hardly modified at all. He is, however, interested to see that the minister, a seasoned politician, has allowed himself to be persuaded over one of the opposition's amendments.

Mr Able has set up a working lunch for one of his local councillors, who will brief him on a particularly difficult local government problem on which he is likely to be presented with a petition. They discuss their tactics for some considerable time, and the member looks at his watch and sees that it is nearly 2.30. He is keen to attend Question Time today, as the questions are to be put to the Home Secretary, from whom he hopes to obtain a public statement on the government's policy on open prisons. His question (which he had to put down two weeks before so as to get it in the Order Paper) is no. 15 and reads, 'Mr Able (Bigley South) to ask the Secretary of State for the Home Department what is the policy of the government with regard to the extension of open prisons'. He knows that the answer will be that the government hopes to build more. Though he thoroughly approves of this, it is not the point of the question. Rather, he hopes to pin the minister down with his 'supplementary', the follow-up question of which the minister will have had no notice. This is both a way of keeping the government on its toes while, at the same time, demonstrating to his constituents that he is active on their behalf. With luck, his supplementary will be reported in the local press.

As Mr Able slips into his seat on the government benches, he sees that the House is full. He has heard that the Secretary of State is going to have a hard time of it. He can already see that a considerable number of backbenchers are waiting to catch the Speaker's eye, jumping up and down in their seats in order to do so.

The events of the afternoon prove that the rumours were correct: the Secretary of State does have a bad forty minutes, but, even so, Mr Able's question is reached at 3.20 p.m. The Speaker calls his name and he stands up. 'Question no. 15, Sir', he says, and waits for the government's expected answer. Now for his supplementary: 'Whilst thanking my right honourable friend for his reply, perhaps he could tell the House why no money had so far been spent on Ainsworth Open Prison, despite repeated statements that this would be forthcoming?' The minister, well briefed by his civil servants, promises that the prison (in Mr Able's constituency) is high on his list of priorities. He has not been floored by the supplementary, as his civil servants had anticipated that Mr Able would be interested in open prisons and had briefed him accordingly. Mr Able is reasonably satisfied, as, at the least, he can in future remind the minister of his promise.

Although he is anxious to get away in order to prepare for the evening's debate, Mr Able decides to stay for a statement which is to be made by the Minister of Transport after Question Time. He had hoped to hear that a proposed new spur of a motorway would cross the north-west part of his constituency. But he is out of luck: the spur is to stop five miles short of the constituency boundary. This will be a disappointment for those who have been lobbying hard for the extension. Mr Able sighs as he sees another time-consuming and probably hopeless fight ahead of him. At least, he thinks, the environmentalists will be pleased. As he leaves the Chamber, he remembers that Mrs Best, an opposition member with a constituency very like his own and therefore with some of the same problems, has won the ballot for the adjournment debate that evening. She is sure to raise some interesting issues, and he decides to stay on after the ten o'clock debate.

Mr Able is one of the lucky members to have an office in the Norman Shaw building in what used to be Scotland Yard. He shares his office with another government backbencher, who, happily for Mr Able, is a lawyer with his own chambers and hardly ever there. However, it does have the disadvantage, since it is on the Embankment, of being a good walk from the Chamber. This in turn means that he has to decide whether he will have time enough to work on his speech if he returns to his office or should work in the Commons Library. He decides to go to his office, make himself a cup of tea and sign the letters which his secretary will have put on his desk. His party committee on the environment is due to meet that day at five o'clock, and he has to make up his mind whether he should attend or miss it and get on with his speech. He will have to return to the Chamber by 5.30 at the latest in order to be in his place long enough to be called by the Speaker.

For a moment he is uncertain what he should do. The advantage of attending the specialist committee is that the minister has agreed to speak to the group and this will give Mr Able an opportunity to discuss some matters of policy and perhaps influence the government, if only at the margin. He hesitates, but reflects that the minister in question is coming to his constituency on an official visit the following week. That will be the time to buttonhole him and explain his views on various issues. Happy to have his quandary solved, he strides out of the Members' Entrance through the underpass which connects Westminster with the Embankment and dashes off to his office for a final look at his speech. He has only a few hours in which to perfect it.

As he reaches his office he hears the telephone ring. It is his secretary informing him that he has agreed to speak at a lunchtime meeting on Saturday in his constituency but that it isn't down on his list of constituency engagements. Also, his wife has 'phoned to confirm that on Sunday they have to go to his parents-in-law and that he must not, therefore, make any extra appointments for that day. Mr Able puts both events in his diary, rings off and gets down to work.

He plans to make a ten-minute speech. He feels that too many members make long speeches which could easily be cut. He hopes that if the Speaker gets to know that he is a man of few but succinct words he will be called in future debates. However, a short speech is far more difficult to make than one which is longer and less precise; so he has already spent some time working on it. This last hour or so he is simply polishing up the final version.

It is a difficult speech to prepare, in the sense that, although he is a firm supporter of the government, he wants to suggest that some of the principles behind the Bill to be debated need to be clarified. He also hopes that some amendments can be made when the Bill is sent upstairs for the committee stage.

Finally Mr Able gathers up his notes and walks briskly back to the Commons. He has not eaten, but there is now no time. As he enters the Chamber, he notices that, as usual, it is nearly empty – about twenty members on the government benches behind the Secretary of State and around the same number on the opposition side. Glancing around, he sees that the colleagues present are all those with a special interest in the Bill. He will see more in the Chamber for the winding-up speech, and even more in the division lobbies for the ten o'clock vote.

He enters the Chamber behind one of his friends just as a backbench opposition Member concludes his speech. Immediately over half the members rise to their feet, waving their papers, Mr Able among them. Not surprisingly, he is not called and settles down to listen to his neighbour, who has been lucky enough to catch the Speaker's eye. The speech is far too long – over twenty minutes – as the angry rustling of papers on the benches opposite indicate. It is now 6 p.m. and Mr Able, having again failed to be called, works out that, if every speech is about fifteen minutes, then only ten more speakers will be called, five of whom will come from the government benches. He is depressed at the thought that all the work and effort he has put in on his speech for the last few days may come to nothing. All the same, each time a speech comes to an end, he jumps up hoping his turn might come.

But it is not Mr Able's night. He is not called. It is therefore with a feeling of deep frustration and depression that he decides not to bother to listen to the winding-up speeches but to have a quick bite to eat before the division. Gloomily he goes off to the members' cafeteria, where he queues for some fish and chips. He wonders as he eats whether the life of a member of Parliament can be anything but frustrating. Reviewing his day, he feels that it has been less than satisfactory: a morning spent unable to open his mouth; a worrying lunch with his constituent; Question Time, which he admits was only partially successful – no money from the government was forthcoming; and a debate in which he had no opportunity to contribute. Hardly a man of power! The only cheerful part of it is that he has managed, in his mail, to solve some constituency problems.

As the division bells begin to ring, Mr Able decides that he will not go to the adjournment debate but go home early. Tomorrow is going to be a full day. A party of local schoolchildren has to be taken around the House and he has promised to write an article for his local paper. There is an environmentalists' pressure group scheduled for noon, and in the afternoon, apart from Prime Minister's Question Time, which he always likes to attend, he has a committee meeting with some councillors over the suggested closure of a school in his area. He also hopes to speak at the weekly party meeting. Perhaps tomorrow he will feel that his job is more worthwhile.

Mrs Best is a young, lively, new member still surprised, given the difficulties that women face in being selected, to have got into

Parliament. Her seat is not absolutely safe, but neither is it, as is so often the case with women, very marginal. It is not too far from London, which has advantages and disadvantages. Whereas Mr Able cannot be expected to attend evening meetings in his constituency, Mrs Best's local party often has no qualms about asking her to address them between the 7 p.m. and the 10 p.m. votes.

Mrs Best's specialisation is education – she was a secondary-school teacher before getting into parliament. Given her interests, she has joined the party's education committee, through which she hopes to be able to contribute to any policy papers which the party may publish.

The day begins badly for Mrs Best. She knows that it is going to be a long one, as she has an adjournment debate that night. But she has also been rung up by the local party secretary and asked to address a rally outside a factory where 500 men have just been given redundancy notices. It is to be a lunchtime meeting, which means that she will probably miss Question Time and also be late for a meeting set up at Westminster with eighty local teachers. Clearly, however, this is an emergency, and of course she will go. Her secretary will have to meet the teachers.

Mrs Best has no office – she simply has a desk in one of the 'cloister end' offices, so that she is surrounded all the time by members walking about, telephoning, being interviewed and generally causing a disturbance. She tends to dictate her letters to her secretary in the corridor leading from the Central Lobby to the Members' Lobby, because, although it is dark, it is usually empty. Today she will not have much time to look at the mail because she wants to attend both her party meeting and the Select Committee on which she serves. She remembers a useful comment on committee work: 'the atmosphere in Committee is different from that of the floor of the House. You have to think twice if you stand up in a Committee. You have to know your stuff. It can be very demanding.' Mrs Best is a member of the Education, Science and Arts Select Committee, which is currently looking into the way in which universities are funded. This is the second meeting on the subject, with oral questions being put that morning to two university vice-chancellors as well as to the Permanent Secretary at the Department of Education and Science (DES).

She enjoys Committee membership. On the whole the MPs on the Committee leave adversarial tactics behind on the floor of the House. They are united in their desire to extract as much information as possible from those who come before them. They are also, of course, expert in their field. Mrs Best decides not to take part in the initial round of questions, as there are a considerable number of members who know more about universities than she does, although she feels that she might have something to contribute later on once a pattern has emerged.

As she suspected, the DES and the vice-chancellors have diffe-rent objectives. The universities want to be left strictly alone; the civil servants want to tighten their hold on them. What the patient questioning of the Committee does bring out is something of which she was unaware, that the DES is working on various funding-schemes which so far have been put forward neither in government statements nor in a government Green Paper. She feels that it has been a morning well spent and intends to use the new information to put down a parliamentary question. She suspects that the government has been trying to bring its policies in through the back door and is determined that it will not get away with it. It is a great pity, she thinks, that not all reports of the Select Committees get the chance to be debated on the floor of the House. It would certainly make the Committees more powerful and, at the same time, force the government to take more notice of their recommendations.

As she dashes to her meeting she meets one of her colleagues, who reminds her that she has promised to come on Friday to take part in the debate on his private member's Bill. He was drawn fifth in the ballot for private members' time and at last his turn has come. It means that she will have to be in the House from 9.30 a.m. to 2.30 p.m. but thinks it is worthwhile. Mrs Best is always anxious that private members should assert their rights as often as possible. She believes that the government of the day can be influenced to some extent if members exert themselves and use all the tools at their command. She rushes into her party meeting. She is keen to see how the leadership is going to answer certain criticisms against its handling of new government proposals on social security. It is felt by a considerable number of opposition backbenchers that the Shadow Cabinet has been too slow to react to the news and that it has allowed the initiative to stay in the hands of the government. She feels strongly, as she slips into Committee Room 10, that there is some truth in the accusation. She herself has just signed an early-day motion on this very subject and has noticed that it contains a considerable number of government backbench signatures. Early-day motions, essentially expressions of opinion, since there will not be time to debate them, are tabled daily in great numbers; they are a way, particularly if members on both sides of the House sign them, of publicly indicating to governments the extent of any disquiet about their policies.

As Mrs Best goes into the room she sees that there is indeed going to be a row. There is a considerable amount of low-level muttering and she can feel the tension in the atmosphere. The Leader, however, sitting at the top table surrounded by his team, looks calm – he is clearly unruffled and is obviously prepared. The shadow social-services spokesman, a tall, very thin woman, looks angry rather than worried. It looks as if the collision is going to be won by the leadership.

And so it proves: the way in which the campaign against the government is going to be conducted is explained, and, although not everyone in the room is completely satisfied, it is obvious that most have been placated. Mrs Best has no time to linger; she is already late for her factory-gate meeting, which is at least forty minutes' drive away.

She wonders if she has time to snatch a sandwich in the cafeteria but decides she has not and is therefore both surprised and grateful when she finds a roll on her desk with a note from her secretary saying that she must not forget to eat it. Quickly she scoops up her briefcase and dashes off to the members' car park.

For once the journey to her constituency is not too bad, so Mrs Best has time to work out what she will say. By the time she arrives at the factory gate she has also decided to write a letter to the appropriate minister, as the government is one of the main customers of this particular factory. The attack has to be waged on as many fronts as possible – a 'private-notice' question, which might draw a ministerial statement, could also be asked. She might even try her luck at Prime Minister's Question Time.

The rally goes off well and afterwards she has time for a short talk with the shop stewards. She has to get back in time for the meeting with the local teachers at 3.30. Had she known beforehand that she would be in the constituency that day, she could have scheduled the meeting there and saved herself some time and effort. She muses that much of her life seems to be like this.

She arrives somewhat breathless in the Central Lobby only a few minutes late. She is sympathetic to the teachers' cause and agrees that they are badly paid. She also agrees to write to the Secretary of State for Education, asking him not to support the closure of one of the schools. She tells the teachers that she will try to fix a meeting with him, but does not hold out much hope.

The teachers keep her for over an hour. After they have gone Mrs Best decides to go to the Library to think about her adjournment debate. She is pleased that her name has come up in the ballot, because she has been anxious for some time to raise a particular topic. She also sees the adjournment debate as another method of putting pressure on the government.

Her adjournment debate is to be after the ten o'clock vote at the end of the day's sitting and will not be expected to be contentious but will be of constituency interest. The government however will have to be prepared to answer for its policies. She will be able to demonstrate to her constituents that she is publicly representing their interests, and she may conceivably secure some small concession, although she knows this is unlikely.

Mrs Best knows that she will only have fifteen minutes to make a speech. She has already told the minister the main points she wishes to make. The substance of the debate will be the closure of two of the largest factories in the constituency; and she now intends to bring in the closure of the third factory, which she has visited that afternoon. She settles down to work determined to finish the speech by 8 p.m., so that she can have some food and then listen to the speeches of the main debate of the day.

Mrs Best keeps to her timetable and by nine o'clock (when she has been working for over twelve hours) is in the Chamber, which is noticeably empty. Both the government and the frontbench opposition speakers are known for the dullness of their delivery, so she is not surprised. Still, she feels that it is worth her while to listen to them, as she hopes one day to be a minister and there are a considerable number of skills which she will have to learn before becoming an effective speaker. It is clear to her that neither spokesman this evening has much to offer, but at least she is learning how *not* to make a speech. By the time the division bell goes, the Chamber has filled up and there is the usual predetermined flow into the Aye and No lobbies. There will be no surprises, as the government has a large majority and there is a three-line whip on both sides – that is, members are expected to vote and not pair. Pairing is a mechanism which allows a member on one side of the House to agree with one on the other side not to vote, so cancelling each other out. In the 1983 parliament, pairing was not allowed by the main opposition party.

Finally the Chamber is almost empty. A government whip moves 'that this House do now adjourn' and Mrs Best's debate has begun. It is rather strange to find herself alone on the opposition side of the House with only the Deputy Speaker, the junior minister and a government whip in attendance. She rises to her feet and begins her speech; fifteen minutes later she has finished. The junior minister replies and that is the end. There is no vote and the House adjourns – with ceremony. The Serjeant at Arms moves up the floor of the House, lifts the Mace, puts it on his shoulder and walks out of the Chamber, followed by the Deputy Speaker. The cry goes up, 'Who goes Home?', followed by 'Usual time tomorrow', and the parliamentary day has ended.

Mrs Best leaves the House relatively satisfied. Given that she is an opposition backbencher, she knows that she can have little influence on the government with its large majority. Nevertheless, she feels that her Select Committee has unearthed what may be seen as underhand dealings on the part of the government, and she is sure that if there is good press coverage the government will have to respond and explain quite quickly. Although she has not taken part in Question Time, she hopes to have some answers to the written questions she has put down to various ministers. These she intends to use as further ammunition against the government.

She is particularly pleased with her adjournment debate. She knows that she will get local coverage, since she has forced the government to admit that it has no intention of giving any financial assistance to her constituency. It will form part of her indictment of the present administration and, she hopes, will assist in its downfall at the next general election.

As she once more walks to the underground car park she realises that she has been on the go for fourteen hours. Tomorrow, she thinks without conviction, may prove to be less exhausting.

5

Pay and Conditions

*When each new Parliament as-
sembles, the new members express
astonishment at the lack of adequate
facilities for the work they hope to
do.*
(Select Committee on House of
Commons Services,
Fifth Report, 1977–8 HC483,
para. 12)

Members' jobs have been increasingly 'professionalised' in the last twenty years, both in terms of their own attitudes and commitment, and in the degree and nature of the support and facilities they now command. The Lawrence Committee report of 1964, which recommended not only substantial pay increases but also a widening in the scope and variety of allowances, is recognisable as something of a milestone in this context.[1] The explicit acknowledgement in the TSRB report of 1971 that a member's job could be full-time and should be paid accordingly carried with it further implications about the level of facilities and services necessary to support them. Not all of these, however, have yet been fully spelled out, still less agreed upon by members themselves and the successive governments which have to budget for them.

PARLIAMENTARY PRIVILEGE

Parliamentary privilege, the body of rights and immunities won in the years when Parliament struggled to establish its independence from the monarch, constitutes perhaps the oldest 'support' for members of Parliament in the performance of their jobs. Members' freedom of speech in debate, freedom from arrest in civil suits, and the right of the House to assert its independence from the crown courts by itself punishing those whom its Committee of Privileges deems guilty of breach of privilege or contempt of the House have been important in the past. They have facilitated and indeed made possible the performance of MPs' jobs. Such privileges are still confirmed to each parliament by the sovereign, but the justification and necessity for them today is now questioned. Geoffrey Marshall, for example, contends that parliamentary privilege 'impinges upon the rule of law and the liberties of the subject when many of the crises and conflicts from which the privileges of Parliament took their present shape are of no present concern'.[2]

These days, the most visible manifestation of members' right to freedom from arrest and, associated with that, from molestation when entering or leaving the Palace of Westminster, may be the Sessional Order authorising police to give priority to members' cars in the streets around Parliament Square.[3] Members' right to immunity from actions for slander for what they say in the House certainly excites controversy today, if allegations are made in the Chamber that could not be made with impunity outside it. In the 1985–6 session, for example, Geoffrey Dickens MP aroused considerable comment when he named in the House a doctor whom, he said, had raped a girl. The Speaker prevented him from similarly naming a vicar who he claimed was guilty of sex offences with children. Since such individuals have no redress unless such allegations are repeated outside the House, the expectation is that members will use their privilege responsibly to avoid injustice, and this is in fact widely respected.

Parliamentary privilege is a sensitive issue for the House, which has so far shied away from codifying or updating it. Facilities and support for members are more usually discussed at the more mundane level of the pay, allowances, accommodation and staffing available to them.

PAY AND ALLOWANCES

Appropriate levels of pay for MPs have long been a thorny issue. The meticulously researched independent assessments of the TSRB have not necessarily been acceptable to cost-conscious governments. The most recent formula for members' pay was confirmed in July 1987, and was a compromise based on the recommendations of the TSRB, which the government would not accept *in toto*. It linked members' pay to a middle ranking civil service grade, in an odd equation, 89% of the top point of the senior principal scale. This betrayed its origins as a compromise, but also yielded members a welcome 22% rise to £22,548 p.a. in January 1988. Such a linkage remains controversial. Can an MP's job really be worth only ¾ of a civil servant's, and not a top one at that? But at least members are not faced with the necessity of being seen by their constituents to be "voting themselves a pay rise", and the formula does at least for a time, as the late Sir Hugh Fraser MP remarked, 'rid the House of this continual and embarrassing debate about whether we should be weighed in diamonds, feathers or lead, like the Aga Khan'.[4] How far the question of members' remuneration can, in reality, ever be withdrawn for long from the arena of political controversy remains doubtful. Allowances are now generous by earlier standards, so much so that critics have called them "iceberg remuneration", supplementing modest salaries. Chief amongst them is the allowance for secretarial, research and office expenses. In July 1986, in one of those occasional rebellions which demonstrate that the House is nobody's poodle, the Commons defeated a government proposal for a modest 6% increase and secured a 52½% rise from £13,211 to £20,140, more even than the TSRB subsequently reported as appropriate in April 1987. This allowance is now linked to the salary of a senior personal secretary in the civil service and once parity with TSRB recommended levels has been reached, will rise with it, subject to reviews every four years. Other allowances were agreed in 1983 for secretaries winding up members' affairs after death or defeat in elections, and for paying temporary staff if secretaries were away for four weeks or more.

In addition, members with inner-London constituencies can claim a London allowance (£1,023 in 1987), while those with constituencies outside London can claim a tax free 'away from home' allowance of up to £9,468 a year in 1989. This last constitutes a *de facto* recognition that for members to do their job effectively they have to spend time in both Westminster and the constituency. Expenses can be claimed when a member has to stay away from his or her main home on parliamentary duties, whether that is in London or the constituency. Monthly claims for accommodation in hotels, lodgings, clubs and hostels can be reimbursed, but the allowance may also be used to pay mortgage interest on second homes either in London or in the constituency. A 1982 survey found that almost a third of members had their main residence in London, that a third had their second home there, and that the rest rented accommodation in town.[5]

Travel on Parliamentary business between Westminster and the constituency (and elsewhere, with notice) by public transport is free. A car allowance of up to 42p a mile, determined by the size of the car, is paid without supporting documentation up to 20,000 miles a year, but is thereafter calculated at reduced rates to 25,000 miles, to a maximum of 50,000 miles which members with distant constituencies tend to find ungenerous. Others, by contrast, say that the new rates encourage the use of large cars. Spouses and children are each entitled to a maximum of fifteen free return journeys to the constituency a year; members' staff, to nine.

PENSIONS

Pensions and severance pay are of particular interest in a profession whose tenure is uncertain, whose skills are largely unmarketable and whose alumni are often unpopular with employers; less than 10 per cent of members who lose their seats succeed in obtaining re-election. Terms are not particularly generous, but do take some account of the special characteristics of the job, and the plight of retiring or defeated full-time members with no other source of income. A survey of members defeated in the 1979 general election illustrates the potential difficulties ex-members can face in re-establishing themselves. Seven (of the 80 per cent responding) found jobs within three weeks of the general election, five were unemployed for over a year, while the mean time taken to find a job was twenty-eight weeks – a long time to be without an income, especially for those with dependent families.[6]

Severance pay is now available to all MPs not standing again or not re-elected, and varies from six months' salary for those under the age of fifty to a maximum of one year's salary for members over fifty-five and with at least fifteen years service. Contributions of 9 per cent of members' salary afford provision for dependents and earn ex-members a full pension of two thirds of their final salary at sixty-five.

Apart from salary and allowances, members get free stationery for parliamentary rather than political or personal use, and free inland telephone and postal services from Parliament. They can obtain free copies of Parliamentary Papers, the daily *Hansard*, and the 'vote bundle', containing the order paper and the votes and proceedings of the House, which can be delivered, if required, to houses within a radius of three miles of the House of Commons. Members who live less than one and a half miles from the House (often in practice senior front benchers, and mostly Conservatives) can have a personal division bell installed in their homes, an amenity which releases them from the tedium of hanging around the House simply in order to obey the three-line whip.

OFFICE EQUIPMENT AND FACILITIES

Members do not get much in the way of modern equipment: filing-cabinets and communal photocopying-machines are available, but members have to supply their own computers, telephone answering machines, fax equipment, word-processors and electric typewriters out of their allowances, or accept the offers of use of computers and equipment made to them by major companies. In the opinion of at least one member, Alan Williams, 'The House of Commons is still at the abacus stage in its application of information technology to its back-up facilities'.[7] The House of Commons Services Committee has proposed that cabling for individual computers should be installed throughout the Commons; centrally provided and standardised equipment could give members word-processing and document reproduction facilities, an electronic mail system such as has already been experimented with in the House, instant access to a variety of sources of information, and perhaps also important, improved communication with the constituency. The problem is not only the cost, but consensus on the proposals. As the Leader of the House put it, '... different members have different views about the speed with which technology should be introduced in this place.'[8]

The adequacy of salaries and allowances has always been a source of disagreement amongst members. Most, especially those who have come to the House from teaching or lecturing, find it adequate; others feel they are not getting the rate for the job but recognise that it is one to which doctrines of 'market forces' cannot be applied, while still others refuse to take their full salary for reasons of their own. Many certainly take a substantial cut in salary on coming into the House. Even those who do not, can find that the unexpected costs of parliamentary life force them to find a second paying job, despite the specific recommendations of successive review bodies that salaries should be set at levels that make this unnecessary. The TSRB found that fully 69 per cent of members reported regular or occasional paid occupations in addition to their parliamentary duties, bringing them in a median additional income of just over a third of their salaries at the time.[9] Certainly, as member Andrew Hunter says, 'Being an MP is an expensive business', and the incidental costs can be high. They include the need to run what can in effect amount to two homes, as well as the unlooked-for cost of providing teas, lunches and dinners, or even just cups of coffee (the cumulative cost can be considerable), to constituents who visit them at the House, and are blissfully unaware or uncaring that the cost of their refreshment comes out of the MP's own pocket, not some expense allowance. One MP has seen his overdraft going up by about £300 a month: 'sometimes I can get through £20 in one evening on raffle tickets, drinks, and fund-raising projects in the constituency which I feel I am expected to support'. Rosie Barnes pointed out, 'I earn just over £20,000, of which £10,000 goes on childminding. By the time I have paid for my drycleaning and kept my clothes up to scratch, I probably take home less than my secretary'.[10]

Some MPs employ their spouses as full- or part-time secretarial and/or research assistants, and incidentally increase the family income in so doing. Roger Gale MP puts up a persuasive defence of the employment of wives by members:

> this is not, as is popularly believed outside the House, a way for a Member of Parliament to enhance his salary. . . . In my experience, most Hon. Members who employ their wives do so at less than those ladies earned before starting to work here . . . it is the only way I can get someone to work for me 17 hours a day, and 6 days a week for the money. It is also the only way that some of us manage to see our wives.[11]

Many members find their spouses are anyway pressed into unpaid service, answering the telephone, fielding problems, taking messages and doing chores in the constituency which go way beyond the usual demands of conjugal loyalty and support. As Richard Holt MP argued, 'some members' wives do many jobs in the constituencies for which they are not remunerated, or paid . . . that aspect should be examined'.[12]

In fact, despite the 'away from home allowance', the allowances are not structured to take full account of the costs of constituency-related work. Members who run offices in their constituencies can incur heavy overheads, including bills for rent, rates, telephone (calls are only free from the Palace of Westminster), copying-machines and other equipment. Running regular surgeries is expensive if rooms have to be hired, and even the advertising of such surgeries can be costly. Even where party or trade union facilities are provided (more often for Conservatives than for others) the trend is towards higher, economic rents. Most MPs would like official assistance in their constituencies for at least offices, equipment, telephones and secretarial help.[13] The sugges-tion increasingly canvassed is that the Returning Officer in each constituency should provide most of these against repayment from the government.[14] Some would like to emulate Ken Livingstone and have their main office in the constituency, because 'all the problems are there', yet the costs exceed even the new allowances, and the balance has to be met out of salary.

SECRETARIAL AND RESEARCH ASSISTANCE

The adequacy of secretarial and research allowances is still much more often questioned and complained about by members than are salary levels. There is, inevitably, no consensus amongst members of Parliament about what kind of or how many staff they need to do their jobs effectively. The traditionalist view is that 'all a good MP needs is a typewriter and a good secretary'. Barry Field MP, for example, declared in November 1987 that 'the employment of research assistants strikes at the heart of parliamentary democracy.'[15] At the other extreme are the members with passes to the House of Commons for no fewer than 14 research assistants and nine secretaries respectively. Seventeen members are recorded as having between four and eight research assistants each, and 34 between three and six secretaries each,[16] though such figures must be treated with some caution, for there is no indication of how many hours such staff work. Roger Gale explains that of his five research-assistant passes, one went to his wife, who was his secretary and personal assistant, two to students from Surrey and London universities who were working on projects, one to a constituency assistant who visits the House some three times a year, and one to an American student on a temporary assignment.[17] It is clear that 'minimalist' attitudes to staff support are on the decline. New members have greater expectations and make greater demands than the older ones, and find that the increasing workload requires greater staff support.

The recommendation of the Top Salaries Review Body is that allowances should be sufficient to enable members to employ one full-time and one part-time member of staff. In a survey in October 1986, before the full effect of the substantial increase in allowances for staffing was apparent, the TSRB found average staff strength amongst members was not far off its recommendation, at 1.2 secretaries and 0.4 research assistants.[18]

Most members do in fact employ at least one secretary at least part-time at Westminster, but there is wide variation in the arrangements for staff support, how it is distributed between the constituency and Westminster, and, indeed, how it is financed. Our survey in 1985 illustrated a range of possibilities. Andrew Hunter had a secretary in the constituency, but none in the House; Charles Wardle had a secretary at Westminster and saw no necessity for a full-time research assistant but used his own secretary from his business in the constituency; Alexander Pollock shared a secretary at Westminster, had part-time secretarial help in the constituency (supplemented by the unpaid help of his wife) and preferred to do his own research; Chris Smith had both a full-time secretary and a researcher in the House, 'unpaid and over-worked', and a part-time typist; Angela Rumbold employed a full-time secretary at Westminster and a constituency secretary, but had no paid research assistant; Ann Clwyd had part-time secretarial assistance in both Westminster and the constituency, paying for one-off pieces of research; Cecil Franks had a full-time secretary in the House, and an agent in the constituency who doubled as a secretary; while Roger Freeman was in the happy position of having a secretary in Parliament, a research assistant paid for by a constituency trust, plus an agent and a secretary in the constituency.

Since 1986 and the increased allowances, an establishment of three part-time assistants seems increasingly popular amongst those relying exclusively on their allowances to finance help. At the same time, increasing constituency requirements, case work, and the need for sensitivity to local political issues and personalities, can mean that members now prefer to employ their 'main' staff in the constituency. Hilary Armstrong does this, and in addition, has secretarial help in Westminster three times a week, while both Gillian Shephard and Graham Allen use two part-timers in the constituency and one in the House. Though James Arbuthnot MP, for one, thinks secretarial and research allowances too high and encourage inflated salaries, and that many members prefer to do their own research anyway, the majority of members we interviewed, new to the House in 1987, complained that even the increased secretarial and research allowances were not enough to cover an appropriate level of research assistance. It may be that members' staffing needs, like their jobs, are 'infinitely expandable.'

Since there is no commonly agreed definition of what 'research' assistance means in this context, it is difficult to assess precisely what assistance members do in practice either use or need, besides that afforded by their secretaries. Differing possible job descriptions for Parliamentary support staff, with appropriate pay scales, have been suggested by the consultants to the TSRB, but not officially taken up.[19] Meanwhile many members' secretaries act as research assistants as well as secretaries; a few research assistants are of such status as to warrant their own secretaries; while many research assistants are really personal assistants helping, as Barry Sheerman put it, with 'photocopying, or the myriad of different jobs that a modern legislator has to undertake'. Much 'research' of the personal-assistant variety has been provided for members by volunteers, often students, foreign and usually American, on 'internship' programmes. Concern in the House at the strain placed on scarce facilities, and especially the Library, by temporary assistants unfamiliar with the basics of how British government works, has led to a limit being placed on the number allowed into the House and employed by any one member.

Some members (and they are more likely to be from the Conservative Party than from the other parties) can afford to pay for extra help personally, or are fortunate enough to be offered the services of research or secretarial assistants financed by the organisations for which they work or with which they have connections. Paul Bryan acknowledged gratefully the help he received in pursuing his interests in Hong Kong affairs: 'The High Commission provides an endless supply of press cuttings, and many other organisations provide any information I need. In the modern world a large number of organisations, trade associations, and trade unions are becoming very good at this kind of work, and a great deal of information can be obtained in this way.'[20] Not all members approve of such arrangements, and Kevin McNamara, for one, argues that it can lead to at least a partial loss of independence.[21] Members can call upon support from other sources. All the parties have research departments which furnish briefs and background papers of their positions on the major and topical issues of the day. The Conservative Party Research Department is considered the Rolls Royce amongst them, and, indeed, employment in that department has been a frequent route into the House and into government for bright and ambitious Tories.

LIBRARY

The Library of the House of Commons is probably members' most often cited and certainly most praised source of information. Its remit is 'to supply members with information rapidly on any of the multifarious matters which come before the House or to which their attentions are drawn by their Parliamentary duties' and it must do so in a politically impartial fashion.[22] No recent debate or report on the services and facilities of the House has lacked reference to the 'excellent Library and first-class research staff'. The paeans of praise are qualified only by concern at the seemingly ever-increasing demands made upon these resources. The Library retains its club-like atmosphere, with leather armchairs grouped around fireplaces and writing-tables arranged in a setting which exemplifies the best of Pugin. Nowadays, however, the Library is amongst the most modern and technologically advanced services in the House. The parliamentary on-line information system, Polis, the computer-based index of parliamentary questions, debates, statements and parliamentary papers, and European Community legislation, is run by the Library's Computer and Technical Services Section, and is a valued aid to members and the staff working for them in finding parliamentary material and other information. Polis is supplemented by a view-data television, with access to a wide variety of data bases. These include TextLine, (which provides press summaries), the Central Statistical Office data base Nomis (which shows unemployment by constituency and even by ward), the teletext services of the Post Office, BBC and IBA, and Blaise (the British Library Information Service).

Such facilities complement extensive holdings of books, parliamentary and reference material, and much-used collections of press cuttings on international and home affairs. Members also have access to the House of Lords Library. Staff of the Parliamentary Division in the main library suite of the Commons are available to give members quick, accurate answers to short, usually oral, enquiries for as long as the House is sitting. The nineteen specialists in the five sections of the Research Division (located in a 'Gulag Archipelago of little bits' around the House), together with the staff of the International affairs section and European Community desk in the Parliamentary Division, usually answer in depth, in writing and in confidence, the more searching, longer-term queries. Research Division staff can help members use the Treasury's macroeconomic computer 'model' of the UK economy, to which members have had access since 1979, and discuss with them the assumptions, implications and interpretations of the simulations carried out on the model. (Members also have access, through the Parliamentary Unit set up at Warwick University, to all the UK national economic models.) Generalised material on topics of current interest and importance, in the form of reference sheets, background papers and research notes, are also periodically produced by the Reference Division.

Demand for the Library's excellent but sometimes hard-pressed services has escalated with the increasing professionalisation of members' jobs. Over a recent ten-year period, the number of enquiries answered in writing by the Research Division and International Affairs section increased by 77 per cent, reflecting in turn the growing workload and changing work patterns of the members, who make some 80 per cent of the enquiries personally, rather than through their research assistants.[23]

Members' secretaries and research assistants have only very limited access to the main House of Commons Library. However, the branch library in Norman Shaw North provides them with substantial reference facilities. It is combined with the Public Information Office, which in a year answers almost 100,000 telephone enquiries both from researchers in the House and from

outside callers. It publishes general background papers called
Factsheets on such basic topics as *The Parliamentary Stages of a
Government Bill*, useful for members' staff and constituents alike –
and often to members themselves. Its Education Service, which is
aimed at schoolchildren, provides tours of the House, videos and
printed material on Parliament, as well as giving members much-
valued assistance with the necessary but time-consuming task of
coping with enquiries about Parliament from schoolchildren in
their constituency, or school parties visiting Westminster.

DEPARTMENTS OF THE HOUSE

The Library is but one of seven departments in the House whose
function is in one way or another to support and help members of
Parliament in the performance of their jobs. The most important is
the small Speaker's Office, whose staff, including the Speaker's
secretary, chaplain, two counsel and a trainbearer, assist the
Speaker both with his ceremonial functions and with his heavy
responsibilities in the Chamber. Very important too are the officials
of the Clerks Department, who act as the House secretariat,
advising members on procedure, as well as administering and
formally recording the business of the House. Clerks in the Table
Office deal with questions, advising members on which are
acceptable and in what form they should be tabled, and then
forwarding them to the relevant government departments to
answer. The Public and Private Bill Offices handle all Bills in the
Commons through all their stages from receipt of the text to Royal
Assent. The Journal Office records the doings of the House rather
than, as *Hansard* does, reporting the debates. It identifies the
rulings and precedents set by the Speaker, which guide proceedings in the Chamber. The Overseas Office deals with foreign
parliaments and international organisations such as the Western
European Union and the Council of Europe, which British members of Parliament attend from time to time, while the Committee
Office clerks administer the increasing number of committees,
including the Select Committees. They arrange for witnesses to be
called and evidence to be presented, make arrangements for
committee visits and draft reports. The clerks' role is to facilitate
the orderly conduct of parliamentary business, but not to influence

its content. Theirs is a low profile, but members collectively and individually would find it hard to operate without their expertise and support.

The Serjeant at Arms' Department maintains and runs the essential services of the House, overseeing security and the administration of Commons premises. Members (or their secretaries on their behalf) apply to the Serjeant for the limited number of passes available for constituents for the Strangers' Gallery; they depend on his department for services as varied as the continued functioning of the overloaded photocopying-machines, the allocation and supervision of the committee rooms, desks and passes for their secretaries and research assistants, and parking-places for their cars. The dignified and tailcoated Badge Messengers, distinguished by their bearing and ability to search out and find the members for whom they carry messages, are in the Serjeant at Arms' Department. In the absence of an individual electronic paging system (the introduction of which would no doubt be resisted by many members), they are a vital means of communication through the miles of corridors and hundreds of rooms of the Palace. The Serjeant himself, besides overseeing the 'housekeeping', performs important and colourful ceremonial duties, but his responsibilities for enforcing order in the Chamber, on the Speaker's direction, are more than merely ceremonial, as members suspended or expelled from the Chamber may find.

A different but equally vital support service to members is provided by the Refreshment Department, which serves food in a variety of cafeterias, dining-rooms and bars (which are not subject to licensing laws) at all hours of the day and night for as long as the House is sitting. They are available either exclusively to members, to members and officers of the House, to members and their guests and/or family, or to staff of the House. Such places as the Tea Room, with its newspapers and salads, traditionally the haunt of Labour members, the panelled Smoking Room favoured by Conservatives and Annie's Bar, where members can drink with journalists, are more than just places of leisure and refreshment. They each have their own atmosphere and contribute to the much-valued and much-vaunted club-like feel of the House, which encourages easy encounters with colleagues, especially in the late evenings as members wait for divisions. In such places members can exchange the information, opinion and gossip which is the life blood of politics and an important part of parliamentary life.

Members can hire the private dining-rooms to host functions for constituency or party groups. Prices, however, are not particularly low, and are subsidised only in the sense that the takings have merely to cover the cost of raw materials.

Of the remaining departments, the Administration Department touches members' working lives in an important way, for its Fees Office pays their salaries and administers their allowances. It also provides them with the opportunity for a personal financial briefing when they first enter the House. The Department of the Official Report produces the record of debates and proceedings, *Hansard*, which is a vital tool for all members, whether for informing themselves or their constituents, or for providing the material for the reports in the local or national press of members' efforts on behalf of the electorate.

In total there are about 1,000 staff employed by the House of Commons itself. In addition there are civil servants and others, not actually employed by the House, who provide important services for members. They include staff from the Department of the Environment and Property Services Agency, who help care for the furnishings and fabric of the building, the Post Office staff, the police, custodians and firemen, and staff of such services as the Transport Office, which arrange members' travel at home and abroad. Their numbers are supplemented by the political, secretarial and administrative staff employed by the whips' offices, and the varying number of part-time specialist advisers appointed to help the Select Committees with their work.

ACCOMMODATION

All these people need to be accommodated with office or at least work space, in a building which, for all its public splendours, was manifestly not designed to hold the numbers who now work there. Some, whose presence is vital to the running of the House, need to be able to spend the night there when the House sits late, and others require more permanent living-space. Mr Speaker has his official residence, with its fine reception rooms for official occasions, in the Palace, and the Clerk of the House has a flat in Norman Shaw South. In all there are said to be some 100 rooms within the precinct of the House of Commons used as residences and bedrooms.

Much of the working-accommodation available to members, their staff and officials is crowded and makeshift; offices are frequently badly lit and airless, and, before the days of the Thames Barrier, were in danger of being flooded by the Thames at high tide. The provisions of the Shops, Offices and Railway Premises Act do not apply to the Palace of Westminster. Members are the tip of the iceberg of people working on the premises, but, naturally, get the better accommodation. Even so, a House Services Committee concluded that 'the majority of accommodation now being used by MPs is substandard, either because of the nature of the historic building or too many people trying to work too closely together'.[24]

Half-a-dozen different schemes for major extensions to meet the burgeoning needs of the House have been shelved in successive expenditure cuts over the last three decades. The latest plan, approved by the House in November 1983, is a scheme for converting premises in Bridge Street to members' use. This will provide up to 85 additional rooms and some improved facilities, such as major new library premises, but the scheme will not be completed until the early 1990s. Acquisitive eyes are cast towards County Hall, the former GLC building just across the river, which could, some members argue, be best employed as a Parliamentary annexe. Meanwhile, attempts to make room in the existing building, by means of expansion, conversion and in-filling, seem to have reached their limits. 'Every possible flat roof has temporary huts on it', groaned the Services Committee.[25] Another recourse has been piecemeal expansion into a variety of available buildings in the vicinity, differing in distance from the Chamber and in character, convenience and charm.

Most accommodation for members outside the Palace is available in the Norman Shaw offices on the Embankment, formerly the headquarters of the Metropolitan Police, Scotland Yard. These handsome buildings contain accommodation that is pleasant, well-furnished, and modern, though often again very crowded. Further accommodation is available near Westminster Abbey, in Old Palace Yard, Dean's Yard, and at 2, The Abbey Garden. Distance from the Chamber (even with the increase in time allowed for divisions since the Norman Shaw buildings were brought into use), the separation from the sometimes electric, and usually compelling atmosphere of the House, and the need to cross busy thoroughfares, especially from the sites near the Abbey, make the outbuildings unpopular with many members, despite their amenities. There are, however, writing-desks in scattered locations about the House, in the division lobbies and in members' lounges, that members whose offices are in outbuildings can use when they are in the House.

Most newcomers, once they have realised how short accommodation is in the Commons, are simply grateful to get any reasonable office space. There is now, after years of making-do and *ad hoc* expansion, at least desk space somewhere in the House of Commons premises for every member who applies for it. Fewer than half can aspire to a room to themselves, and not many rooms in the Palace itself are available to backbench newcomers. Over 400 members can now be 'accommodated' there, but accommodation is somewhat minimally defined as 'space for a desk, and a filing cabinet'.[26] Ministers, opposition frontbenchers and senior members such as the chairmen of the Select Committees are given preference for the single rooms, which are allocated by the whips with a patronage and slowness often unpopular with the younger members. One of the fortunate backbenchers of 1987, Graham Allen, went to see his Whip 'every hour on the hour' for a fortnight, and even wrote him a poem before landing his prize. His colleague Ken Livingstone, however, fed up with drifting about the Commons corridors 'like some medieval ghost' withdrew from the House to operate from his constituency office, in protest at being 'the only MP without an office at Westminster 322 days after the election'.[27] Only 273 members have private rooms anywhere in the Commons; 242 share double rooms; 30 share with two others; 32 with three; and 62 share with four or more others. 11 members, for reasons of their own, have not claimed accommodation.[28] Privacy, even sufficient peace in which to work, is at a premium under the crowded conditions in the multiple-occupancy rooms, though the differing work habits and timetables of members can make for effective 'coxing and boxing' which can render the conditions more tolerable. Members with desks in what amount to corridors complain that it is hard to deal with some constituency cases with sufficient confidentiality. Conditions are cramped. As Tony Banks put it graphically, 'there are larger lavatories in County Hall than there are rooms in the cloisters in which we work'. 'We have 5½ square yards of working space,' complained a colleague, 'and we must stand on top of the writing desk to open a window.'[29]

The accommodation available for MPs' secretaries and research assistants is scarce indeed, and very little of it, of course, is situated conveniently near the MPs themselves. There are nothing like enough desk spaces anywhere in the buildings to give each member at least one desk to be shared by the notional one and a half staff supposed to be covered by allowances. In 1987, when the total number of full-time and temporary secretaries and research assistants with passes to the Palace was 1151, there were only 422 desk spaces available to staffers, very few in private rooms, with the expectation that 30 more would become available in 1, Cannon Row, and 100 in the new Bridge Street building when completed.[30] A waiting-list for desks is maintained by the Serjeant at Arms' Department, and secretaries employed by more than one MP register desks in the name of both or all of the members they work for to ensure that they keep their desk if they stop working for one of them for any reason.

Members complain bitterly about the 'dire waste of time' involved in trekking between the House and their desks or those of their staff outside the Palace. Roger Freeman, for one, saw the separation of secretaries from the members for whom they worked as the biggest problem posed by accommodation shortages. The introduction of a computer network within the precincts of the Commons could well alleviate that problem, but will not eliminate it until a generation of totally computer-literate members and secretaries emerge, and perhaps not even then.

Questions about the adequacy or otherwise of staff support are intimately related to pressures on the limited accommodation, which have a profound and, in the view of many members, an unwelcome and unjustifiable effect on what back-up facilities they can call upon, and therefore on the work styles which have to be adopted. Churchill's dictum justifying the rebuilding of the Chamber as it had been before it was bombed – 'as we shape our buildings, so they shape us' – has a now unwelcome truth about it for his parliamentary successors.

It would be hard to rival the Terrace at its best, in the sun and without the crowds of members' summer visitors. Indeed, James Arbuthnot lists 'standing on the Terrace with a Pimms discussing the Gulf crisis with the Minister' amongst the compensations of the job. Lounges such as the Harcourt Room and the Members' Guest Room are also very pleasant but despite the eccentric working hours of the House, and the sometimes tedious late-night hours members and staff have to spend there, the facilities for rest and recreation (outside the bars) are not lavish. There are facilities for watching television, three rooms with televisions permanently tuned to one channel each, and facilities for running video recordings. There is a barber shop, and bath and changing rooms – all with a distinctly traditional and masculine flavour – where members can 'freshen up' after an all-night sitting. However, 'there is only one iron and ironing-board in the place', as Angela Rumbold has noted, no ladies' hairdresser, as Ann Clwyd complains nor, until the Bridge Street building opens, anywhere where Members can buy essential groceries. The only game for which provision is made is chess, though there is a rifle range in the basement of the Palace. Members can work off tensions more conventionally and exercise more vigorously by swimming in the RAC pool in Pall Mall – scarcely, however, within the division-bell distance. There is a sun-ray lamp, and at a price, they can use the gymnasium in Norman Shaw North, equipped with 'barbells, and dumb-bells, static bicycles, wall units and a jogging-machine', a sauna and refreshment facilities. The gymnasium is open to spouses of members, who are also allowed access to some of the facilities, such as the Strangers' Cafeteria and the Pugin Room, with guests and without members, but few concessions are made to the fact that most members have families and children. There is now one members' family room, furnished with a TV set, newspapers and magazines, and changing and washing-facilities, available for use by members' parents, brothers, sisters and children, as well as spouses, but it does not – perhaps fortunately, for those who do use it – seem very popular. There is as yet no crèche provided for members or staff with young children, who might find such a facility helpful. The Services Committee 'roundly rejected' a proposal to include one in the plans for Norman Shaw North, whilst approving the inclusion of the gymnasium, TV interview rooms and a flat for the Clerk of the House.[31] Members and their children can, however, get married and have christening services in the House, in the Crypt Chapel. Members can now aspire to a parking-place in or near the House, and spouses may use members' spaces in their stead – a concession the value of which is best illustrated by the scarcity of parking-spaces; there are but twenty places available for members' secretaries, and then only for those 'who have 15 years' service in the House, at the discretion of the Serjeant at Arms'.

Critics of the facilities available to members concentrate on the working environment and are vociferous and numerous; newcomers are especially critical. 'I have not recovered from my initial shock at the appalling working conditions that Members of Parliament have to endure in this place', said Tony Banks. 'The Palace of Westminster is a seedy, run down and thoroughly useless working environment.'[32] Others of the 1983 and 1987 intakes agree that accommodation is 'ludicrous and totally inadequate'. In debates on a number of occasions, members have drawn unfavourable comparisons with the facilities available to foreign legislators 'Compared with any legislature in any civilised country this legislature is appalling'.[33]

Comparisons of UK salaries and facilities with those of US congressmen are of doubtful validity, because of the constitutional and size differences between the two countries, and international comparisons of any sort are difficult because so many elements of allowances and services are differently structured. In a 1986 update of a study he and Thomas Stark made for the 1983 TSRB report, Michael Rush found, despite the increases since then, that in salary terms, compared to their counterparts in broadly similar countries (Australia, Canada, New Zealand, the Federal German Republic, France, Italy and Ireland), British members came seventh out of eight, and compared favourably only with Ireland. In respect of allowances, facilities, and services, legislators in Canada, the Federal Republic of Germany, France and the European Parliament were clearly better off than British members, whereas the Australian, Irish, Italian and possibly New Zealand MPs were worse off. The massive increases in British allowances in 1986 only narrowed the gap between British MPs and more fortunate colleagues. What British MPs lacked most significantly in comparison with the others was specific assistance for the constituency. The full effect of Members' improved capability to employ staff, and the patterns of staff use, are not yet fully established, but it does seem that many members are putting their additional resources into the constituency, both because the perceived needs are there, and also perhaps because the crowded Westminster environment and high London salaries discourage their deployment. Even so a number of members would like yet more assistance in the constituency, not only in terms of standardised facilities provided by Local Authorities, but including staff. Graham Allen's intriguing suggestion was that MPs should have a civil servant assigned to them in the constituency to run the office and deal with all non-political matters.[34]

It may be disconcerting to old hands to find that even after the increases in allowances, some new members are asking for more. It would, however, be a mistake to assume, as we have seen, that the reformers speak for all their colleagues, or, indeed, that there is unanimity even amongst newcomers on the level of support they would like to see. Tom Sackville, as a 1983 entrant, did not count himself amongst the 'frustrated corporate executives who say they need a big room, a computer, and a PA'. Others admit that 'sharing a room can have advantages, in that the novice MP is able to discuss his views with those who have more experience'. Tim Yeo makes the intriguing point that the work style imposed by current conditions in the House is that of the profession which predominates there – the lawyers and barristers, who tend to work alone with their staff situated at some distance. Their work is such that it doesn't need either facilities or staff in order to respond quickly to a daily stream of problems, so they tend to be a group comfortable with the *status quo* at Westminster. It is also true that longer-serving members tend, perhaps inevitably, to have less radical views about improvements, perhaps because they have developed a satisfactory work style within existing conditions and have what the 'young Turks' would call low expectations. John Biffen, as Leader of the House, articulated a not uncommon view amongst the senior members about back-up staff. 'The idea', he said, 'that to do our job we must be buttressed by a growing army of well paid or unpaid research assistants is just one of the current fashions.'[35]

Each intake seems more critical of the conditions at Westminster, and increasingly, of the level of support MPs can call upon in the constituency, than does the one before it. This reaction reflects the changing nature of the job, an increasing workload at Westminster (where the Select Committees and the necessity for scrutinising European legislation have made extra demands on staff and accommodation) and the demands now made on members by constituency 'welfare' work. Westminster has been modernising, but more slowly than many MPs have wished. Workloads have been increasing more quickly than modern methods have been applied to cope with them. Computers, in particular, have been introduced rather late in the day. Successive House of Commons Services Committees, speaking for MPs, have marshalled convincing evidence and made balanced and persuasive recommendations for the improvements which should be made. In the end, however, when it comes to financing improvements, whether of the accommodation, which is so restricting and unsatisfactory, or of allowances for members to employ much-needed staff, unless backbenchers are prepared to stage a revolt, it is governments which decide. They cannot be expected readily to increase expenditure in a less than popular cause especially in times of economic difficulty, particularly if it has the effect of arming the opposition or awkward backbenchers. Members will probably never, in the nature of things, attain the support facilities they regard as ideal, even if they agree on what constitutes the ideal. Changes in pay, allowances and conditions themselves alter the job which MPs can do. The increased allowances of 1986, for example, add a potential new dimension to the job of an MP, that of an employer. The management and administrative implications of such a role, however embryonic, will certainly be unfamiliar to many members, and probably unwelcome to more.

NOTES

1. *Report of the Committee on the Remuneration of Ministers and Members of Parliament*, Cmnd 2576 (HMSO, 1964).
2. G. Marshall, 'The House of Commons and its Privileges', in S. A. Walkland (ed.), *The House of Commons in the Twentieth Century* (Oxford University Press, 1979), p. 204.
3. See Peter Richards, *The Backbenchers* (Faber and Faber, 1972), p. 186.
4. *HC Deb.*, 46, col. 286, 19 July 1983, quoted in D. Judge, 'The Politics of MPs' Pay', *Parliamentary Affairs*, 37, no. 1 (1984) 72.
5. See A. Mitchell, *Westminster Man: A Tribal Anthropology of the Commons People* (Methuen, 1982) p. 185ff.
6. *Review Body on Top Salaries: Report no. 20, Review of Parliamentary Pay and Allowances*, Cmnd 8881 (1983) II 'Survey of the Circumstances and Views on Severance Arrangements of Members of Parliament defeated at the 1979 General Election', p. 58.
7. *HC Deb.*, 82, col. 1394, 12 July 1985.
8. *HC Deb.*, 88, col. 19, 7 Dec. 1987.
9. *Review Body on Top Salaries: Report no. 20*, II, 'Survey of the Circumstances of Members of Parliament and their Views on their Remuneration', pp. 4–5.
10. *Sunday Times Magazine* A Life in the Day of Rosie Barnes, 21 Feb 1988, p. 90.
11. *HC Deb.*, 82, col. 1421, 12 July 1985.
12. *HC Deb.*, 64, col. 650, 20 July 1984.
13. 'House of Commons All Party Reform Group: Findings of MPs'

Attitudes to Reform and the Role of the MP', tabulated by Darren Marshall (unpublished MS, n.d.).

14. See *Review Body on Top Salaries: Report no. 24*, Cmnd 131–II, pp. 42–5.
15. *HC Deb.*, 10 Nov. 1987.
16. See Select Committee on House of Commons Services, *Second Report, 1984–5*, HC 195; and *HC Deb.*, 82 col. 509W, 12 July 1985.
17. *HC Deb.*, 82, col. 1421, 12 July 195.
18. *Review Body on Top Salaries: Report no. 24*, Cmnd 131–II, p. 3.
19. Ibid., pp. 59–73.
20. *HC Deb.*, 82, col. 1416, 12 July 1985.
21. *HC Deb.*, 90, col. 1053, 29 Jan 1986.
22. Quoted in M. Rush, *The House of Commons: Services and Facilities 1972–1982 (Policy Studies Institute, 1983), p. 47.*
23. See *HC Deb.*, 84, col. 660, 28 Oct 1985, and 82, col. 1406, 12 July 1985.
24. Select Committee on House of Commons Services, *Fifth Report, 1977–8*, HC 483, para 34, quoted in Rush, *House of Commons Services and Facilities*, p. 378.
25. Select Committee on House of Commons Services, *Fifth Report, 1977–8*, para. 37.
26. 1982 figures from Rush, *House of Commons Services and Facilities*, p. 82.
27. See *The Independent*, 29 April 1988; Livingstone protest over lack of office.
28. *HC Deb.*, 82, col. 508, 12 July 1985.
29. *HC Deb.*, 64, col. 646, 20 July 1984.
30. *HC Deb.*, 122, c389W 16 Nov. 1987 and *HC Deb.*, 120 c393W 23 July 1987.
31. Rush, *House of Commons Services*, p. 76.
32. *HC Deb.*, 64, col. 638, 20 July 1984.
33. See *HC Deb.*, 90, col. 1047, 29 Jan 1986.
34. *Review Body on Top Salaries: Report no. 20*, II, 116–28, *and Report no. 24*, II, 89–100.
35. *HC Deb.*, 82, col. 1391, 12 July 1985.

6

The Job outside the House

> *Constituency cases . . . illustrate the*
> *reality of politics in a way that is*
> *salutary for members. . . . The cases*
> *are often a useful reminder of how*
> *awful government can be.*
>
> (Mark Fisher MP)

> *We are not crooks*
> (James Prior MP)

IN THE CONSTITUENCY

Parliament may be the main focus and chief workplace for most members, but it is far from the only one. Parliamentary and political duties can take them far afield and occupy a lot of time. When the House is sitting, the mean of the hours members spend on their duties away from the House each week is more than 23. Nearly 7 are spent doing 'preparatory work' for Parliament, 2.5 on a variety of miscellaneous tasks, and nearly 14 on constituency business.[1] The constituency and the affairs of individual constituents can never be too far from their minds, and they themselves cannot be too long away from either. The days when any MP could make one grand annual visit to the constituency are long gone. It is not enough for members to cut a great figure in the House; though the televising of proceedings could help some of them gain a national reputation. Helpful though that can be at election time, it will not, on its own, save members from deselection or from rejection at the polls. Even Cabinet ministers, as we have already seen, take great care to keep up their relationship with the constituency.

Electors, and still more the party faithful, expect to see their member of Parliament and to have easy and reasonably frequent access to him or her. It is important that they feel that their member has a good understanding of and commitment to local issues and concerns. A long-standing connection with a constituency is frequently regarded as an advantage by selectors, and the question 'Will you have a home in the constituency?' is a common one at selection interviews. It is a brave or confident candidate who does not promise to establish a base of some sort in or near the constituency. Quite often, of course, members' families settle, or are already settled, there, and this can be a considerable practical help to the MP, especially if the spouse is willing to help in an official or unofficial capacity (paid or unpaid) with the job. An extra pair of eyes and ears, and a personal representative of the closest kind to make the occasional speech, or fill in for the member when detained in London by parliamentary business, can be very useful, and may even produce electoral benefits. Members with constituencies far from London are perhaps especially conscious of the need to be seen in the constituency. They cannot afford to be known as absentee MPs, always in London.

The argument for assiduous cultivation of the constituency is not merely that it may improve the chance of re-election. Indeed, in Britain electors tend to vote on national issues, and the personality and reputation of individual MPs is not generally considered by analysts to be worth more than some 1500 votes in normal circumstances.[2] Yet in marginal seats it is clearly worth working hard to win the personal vote, and even in 'safe' seats this is always worth securing. In all types of seat too, Labour members, facing, as they now do, rigorous reselection procedures, neglect their local party and constituents at their peril. The job in the constituency is about more than votes and reselection, however. If members are to function properly at Westminster and to serve their party and their country usefully, they must be in touch with conditions and 'grass roots' opinions in the part of the country they represent. They act as two-way channels of information, to the government and the party policy-makers on what the nation thinks and will tolerate, and to the electorate on how government or party policies are to be understood and justified. Strength of feeling amongst members or Parliament, itself influenced by the opinions of constituents expressed in letters to members and through personal contact, can have a powerful effect on policy-makers in government or opposition. Their experience in the constituency talking to 'ordinary' people, dealing with individual cases, perhaps involving hardship, maladministration or injustice, gives members their own sense of how policies work out in practice, and of how well or badly government is working. Even if they see it as their primary role to 'contribute to the national debate' or to act as a 'check on the executive', rather than to be a 'welfare officer' in the constituency, members cannot neglect constituency opinion, or the experience of individual constituents, if they are to fulfil those roles well. To be effective at the national level, MPs need to know their 'patch'. Mark Fisher made the point this way: 'Constituency cases of the social-work variety illustrate the reality of politics in a way that is salutary for members. On the Treasury Committee, relating to billions, it is impossible to feel it as personal. The cases are often a useful reminder of how awful government can be.'

Since the Bill of Rights, one of the historic functions of parliaments has been 'the redress of all grievances'.[3] It is from this ancient right that the differing roles of the modern member in the constituency, as welfare officer, local ombudsman and promoter of local interests, derive. Concern to protect and advance the interests of ordinary citizens and defend them against such administrative, social or financial injustices and hardship as befall them has a long tradition. It must certainly be counted part of the job, and for many backbenchers becomes the main job. The sheer volume of constituency cases generated by economic circumstances was noted by the TSRB in 1983, and increasingly compels members' time and attention, especially if their constituencies are in depressed areas. Some consciously resist being taken over by the constituency aspect of the job, but others come to relish it as the most rewarding part.

Working in the constituency on 'social-work' and local-interest cases can yield considerable personal satisfaction. Ambition for government office and a high profile in policy-making are, after all, only two amongst the many reasons why members are attracted to politics. Notions of public service and a sincere concern for the welfare of their fellows are also strong motivations for many, and find considerable fulfilment in service at the constituency level. 'One of the pleasures of the work is being effective for constituents' is a view reiterated again and again. Members of Parliament do have a certain local cachet which is valuable in problem-solving. 'It's gratifying to be able to move things just by giving a 'phone call and saying "it's the MP" – you don't have to come down like a ton of bricks; people are generally helpful.' Frederick Silvester gave an example from his experience of the sort of result members can sometimes achieve by a simple intervention at constituency level. He was holding a surgery when a man walked in protesting at the slow progress of his industrial-injury case, which had dragged on for four years without result. The member's phone call to the solicitor involved got the case moving immediately and, as Silvester says, four minutes of his time remedied the inefficiency and frustration of four years. New members express surprise at how effective they can be in the constituency, and some clearly enjoy becoming known as local figures in their own right, rather than as purely political figures identified with their party. The feelings of being effective, well known and perhaps popular can be addictive, providing a further reason why some members, especially backbenchers and the new MPs, opt to concentrate on the constituency and the welfare-officer role. It is more difficult to achieve a comparable sense of useful-ness and importance in the House, especially as a new junior member.

Even if they do not live there, most members visit their con-stituency at least once a fortnight. Those with families living there, especially if they have constituencies which are too far away for mid-week visits, may well stay from Thursday night to Monday or even Tuesday morning. Members with constituencies in or near London, on the other hand, may spend a couple of hours working in their constituencies most days, popping back from the House for lunchtime or early-evening meetings with party workers, con-stituents with problems, or local pressure groups. Members with constituencies within easy reach of London may go to the con-stituency for important meetings or events mid-week; but the demands of the whips and the parliamentary timetable generally make them reluctant to accept firm engagements ahead of time. Once there, the range of members' work-related activities in the constituencies is vast; almost everything they do can have rele-vance, albeit indirectly, to some aspect of their job. They are always on show and are regarded by their constituents as public property. If they live in the constituency, they may be called upon at all hours of the day and night, and MPs in this situation often feel harassed. Said one, 'There are always a couple of calls after the pubs close.' And another added, 'The triviality of the problem is often in direct correlation to the insistence of the caller; the ones who telephone you at 8 a.m. on Sunday morning are frequently calling about something quite insignificant. . . .'

SURGERIES

Nearly all members hold regular surgeries in various parts of the constituency, generally on Friday nights and Saturday mornings. Many are held in party offices at central points, but, particularly in far-flung rural areas, some members run mobile surgeries and advertise them in the local press; keen 'social-worker' members even make house calls to constituents they know to have problems. The surgeries are times for listening and for dispensing sympathy and advice. Constituents come to air their political views as well as their problems, and to solicit those of their member on issues of both local and national importance. Most of all constituents come to the member as a person of perceived authority who can help them when they need influential and informed intervention to break through bureaucratic barriers. The range of problems encountered can be daunting; all human life is there, reflecting an often depressing catalogue of misery, inadequacy and bureaucratic failure. Problems vary from the tragic to the absurd, from domestic upsets to questions involving local economic development and amenities, which are often a microcosm of national concerns. Housing and social security cases tend to be most numerous, but a high proportion also concern hospitals and the police. A senior and experienced backbench member estimated that constituency cases (and not all of these emerge in the surgeries; some come to light through letters to members at Westminster) split into about 75 per cent individual cases, 15 per cent policy cases, and the rest problems of 'mechanics' or administration. He also reckons to have an overall success rate of 55–60 per cent in dealing with them.

Sometimes problems are eased on the spot by the provision of a useful address, or help with the drafting of a letter. Often they can be dealt with effectively in the constituency, simply with a 'phone call; sometimes with the help of voluntary organisations, often in co-operation with officials in local offices of central government departments or with local government officers or councillors. Indeed, some members work very closely with local councillors, who may even sit in with them on their surgery. However, there can also be tension and jealousy about central/local government areas of responsibility. Many matters, such as most housing and education grievances, should properly go to local councillors for their attention and are not, strictly speaking, the concern of members of Parliament. Members who have themselves had experience of local government in their constituency agree that they attract a large number of cases because they are well known, and they can also often deal with them successfully because they know the ropes. The more intractable problems may well involve work at Westminster, of the sort discussed in Chapter 3.

Cases which the member feels involve maladministration can be referred to the Parliamentary Commissioner for Administration (the Ombudsman) for an independent assessment of the case, and possibly, ultimately, a recommendation for compensation.

The office of Ombudsman, as Richard Crossman put it when the House was debating the establishment of this office, puts 'at the disposal of the backbench member an extremely sharp and piercing instrument of investigation'.[4] The public have no direct access to him with their complaints, which may only be chanelled through members of Parliament. MPs will only forward a case if they see it is an appropriate one for him to deal with, and if they cannot deal with it themselves in the usual way. The Ombudsman investigates complaints on members' behalf very thoroughly, and often takes a long time to do so. He reports his findings to the MP who referred the case (with a copy the MP can forward to the complainant), and to the head of the department concerned. The MP and the complainant (who need not necessarily be the MP's constituent) decide whether or not to make the findings public. In fact the Ombudsman is not used as much by members as had been expected when the office was set up. The terms of reference of his office are quite strictly tied to maladministration, and the complaints members receive tend often to be about unwelcome administrative decisions rather than maladministration. Nevertheless, it is a useful additional weapon in members' armoury as they seek redress of legitimate grievances and check the executive. The more deprived the constituency in socio-economic terms, the more constituents will tend to come to see their member rather than write to him. It is easier, too, for constituents in the towns to get to surgeries. In the nature of things this tends to mean that surgeries bring Labour and centre parties' members a greater case load than Conservatives who generally represent more affluent, often rural areas. David Alton, member for Liverpool, Mossley Hill, making a plea in the House for greater staff support, gave an idea of the scale of the caseload generated in his surgery: 'last Saturday morning I began at a school in Liverpool at 10 a.m. and finished late in the afternoon, having dealt with dozens of cases and met more than 70 constituents with problems which all need to be followed up'.[5]

PROMOTING THE CONSTITUENCY

'Welfare-officer' work is only one aspect of the job in the constituency. Members may be concerned with every aspect of life in the area, local amenities, local history and tradition, the environment, and development of the economic infrastructure. They will probably be involved in trying to resolve the problems which result when such interests conflict – when, for example, a planned new road or by-pass threatens a historic site or area of outstanding beauty, or where local planning decisions are contested. The local MP can also act as a combined high-level entrepreneur, consultant and public-relations officer, promoting the constituency and its interests in the country and, indeed, the world at large. The furthering of local economic and commercial interests can bring a considerable workload, especially in depressed areas. It can involve trying to bring new industries to the area, refurbishing the old, and helping find new sources of capital for local industrial and commercial development. It can mean working with local industry and trade unions to promote, develop or even merely maintain local employment. Energetic MPs can act as a stimulant to local business, helping to put together joint and co-operative enterprises, advising on government programmes to aid industry and small businesses, and working with other MPs to put together regional initiatives. They can be a source of useful contacts outside the constituency, in London and even abroad, for local interests and local community and business leaders. This kind of role, promoting and protecting wider local interests, tends to appeal to Conservative members, while the 'welfare-officer' role has tended to be favoured by Labour members.[6]

While self-promotion may not be a primary aim in any of these activities, it would clearly be unduly modest, as well as unwise, for MPs to hide their light under a bushel and neglect to let their

constituents and supporters know of all this activity on their
behalf. Most members are concerned to get publicity in the local
press. Not all are as organised and systematic about it as the
member who routinely dealt with his letters about local problems
as well as surgery cases in the constituency, and spent time on
Mondays and Fridays with his agent at the site of problems, being
photographed and issuing press releases about them.

Politics, and party affairs in particular, may also claim a significant amount of members' time in the constituency. Canvassing
will be necessary where majorities are small, while party branch
meetings, social functions, fund-raising drives and meetings with
the agent are all a necessary part of securing the home base.

PROMOTING THE MEMBER

Most members make every effort to get out and about in the
constituency, going to the places where they can meet a wide
range of people, trying all the time to be affable, approachable,
effective and persuasive. As one remarked, the surgery cases bring
them into contact with constituents who are, on the whole,
atypical.[7] Another important part of the job in the constituency is
to become known to those without dire problems who make up the
majority of the electorate. Saturday morning in a rural constituency
may take the member to the market-place. Sean Hughes MP finds
he spends a lot of time usefully visiting the local gaol! Visits to
hospitals, old people's homes, school and church functions and
charitable associations feature to some extent in the programmes of
virtually every member.

Roger Gale's constituency diary for a typical January and February illustrates the range of engagements in the constituency
undertaken by a hard-working new backbench member. It includes
appointments for surgeries in different parts of the constituency,
house calls, casework meetings with officials in local social-
service departments and with local education officials; visits to the
Travel Extravaganza in the Winter Gardens, Margate, to a Herne
Bay Operatic Society production and to a concert for senior
citizens; inspection of a local sewage works, and a visit to Canter-
bury gaol; tea parties for the mentally handicapped, and, at his
own house, for the Thanet Phobic Trust; meetings with Young

Conservatives, a ward AGM, and a wine and cheese party; attendance at a Blessing of the Seas ceremony and at the induction of a new parish priest; a Greek Community evening; a meeting with Thanet opticians; visits to business enterprises; a talk to the local Chamber of Commerce; visits to no fewer than fifteen schools of different sorts; a dinner dance for the Royal National Lifeboat Institution, and attendance and participation at the new BMX track of the Herne Bay Flyers Roller Speed Club. The diary also shows Roger Gale's wife, who works closely with him, taking the 'representational' role still often expected particularly of Conservative members' wives, at club lunches and ward meetings.

TRAVEL

Constituency work can take members abroad – for example, on a goodwill visit to represent a major town in the district in a town-twinning ceremony, or on a mission to raise money for the area from the European Community. The tiring, sometimes gruelling, pattern of commuting between Westminster and the constituency relaxes in the recesses, when members can take time off or even spend more time in the constituency. Most go on holiday with their families in August. The Westminster-constituency axis can be varied even in the course of the session (with the agreement of the whips), by party and parliamentary duties elsewhere. Party obligations can involve members in canvassing and speaking in different parts of the country at any time – for example, in support of party colleagues in by-elections. The party conferences, often held in seaside towns, are an annual fixture for most members towards the end of the summer recess. Parliamentary delegations to other countries, to celebrate notable anniversaries and to bear fraternal greeting to other democratic legislatures, can provide a break from the usual pattern too. Meetings abroad of such organisations as the British-American Parliamentary Group are timed as far as possible for the recesses, but travel on official parliamentary business (as, for example, with a Select Committee) may have to take place during the session. Select Committee business can involve a fair amount of travel, to destinations of widely varying glamour and desirability. In a typical session, members of the various Select Committees went on a total of 42 fact-finding trips around the

United Kingdom and on 18 abroad. The 18 members of the Delegation to the North Atlantic Assembly, and the 32 members included in the Delegations to the Council of Europe and the Western European Union, have regular opportunities to travel to Paris and Strasbourg, and occasionally further afield. The members of such delegations tend to be senior members chosen by the Whips. Some 70 per cent of MPs go abroad on parliamentary business of one sort or another, and spend a mean of 18 days a year in this way.[8]

OUTSIDE PROFESSIONAL COMMITMENTS

The MP's job outside the House does not extend only to time spent in the constituency or on party business, participating in delegations and conferences. Many members also see the experience they gain as consultants or professional people as crucial to their parliamentary role. The argument is often made that MPs without contacts beyond Westminster are not able adequately to represent feeling in the country and that the political cocoon of the House of Commons induces a debilitating myopia in those 'professional' MPs who pride themselves on never taking an outside job. The split in opinion here is largely a party one: the Conservatives, who tend to be business or professional people, defend the right of the MP to maintain outside contacts, while many Labour members disparage the 'part-timers' as dilettantes. Says Conservative Colin Shepherd, 'I made it clear from interview for selection onwards that I considered it essential to have an outside business interest.' Labour's Dennis Canavan, however, believes that 'Full-time commitment is required if the job is to be done properly', and he thinks there should be legislation to limit outside interests. John Cartwright, of the SDP, in the House for more than twelve years, says he has modified his view somewhat in that time: 'I'm rather less arrogant about part-timers than I used to be. I thought it was an insult to suggest the political job didn't need all your time, but, against that, the House needs the experience and widespread interests of its members and those with such contacts make a real contribution.'

Whatever individual members may think, the Top Salaries Review Body has found that nearly 70 per cent of MPs had paid jobs, regular or occasional, outside the House. (This figure is, of course, partly a reflection of the high number of Conservative members in the House at the time.) These range from professionals – accountants, bankers, lawyers and businessmen – who keep up their links with their erstwhile employers, as consultants or members of boards, to those whose media connections bring them the odd bit of television or journalism. Clearly, some jobs fit in with political life better than others: it may be particularly easy for a member to keep up with business connections in the City in the mornings and adjourn to the House in the later afternoon or early evening. Similarly, it is possible for well-established lawyers to practise while maintaining their parliamentary careers. It is not, however, possible to continue as a primary-school teacher or a social worker while doing the MP's job, and people from such backgrounds form the backbone of those with no 'outside' involvements.

There has always been a relatively high, and constant, proportion of lawyers (those with legal training, whether practising or otherwise) in national politics, not just because the hours of the House may allow them to continue to practise their profession, but also because the experience gained in the legal sphere – of representing people, arguing cases, public speaking, and so on – is clearly helpful in the political one. Since 1945, lawyers have consistently made up between 15 and 18 per cent of the membership of the House of Commons. Over the same period, teachers (including both the school and university sectors) have also made up a high proportion of MPs, but, whereas the majority of lawyers are Conservatives, the majority of teachers are Labour members.[9] In 1983, over a quarter of the Parliamentary Labour Party (25.8 per cent) came from teaching backgrounds.[10] This suggests that the Labour Party's general view of 'outside involvements' as suspect is at least partly a result of their not being so readily employable as their Conservative colleagues in business or the law. Andrew Hunter, a Conservative ex-schoolteacher, seems to confirm this when he says, 'I need an outside job but it's difficult to find with my background and no business or City connections.'

Hunter's comment here underlines the consideration most likely to influence members in their choice of outside occupations – money. For those who were schoolteachers or political researchers before they entered the House, the backbench salary compares fairly well with what they were earning before. For the merchant banker, this is clearly not so and he will have the opportunity to 'top up' from his outside involvements. It is clear, too, that there will always be MPs who realise that their political careers are insecure and that it would therefore be naïve and premature of them to sever their professional connections. Many of the Conservatives we talked to put themselves in this category, several agreeing that they might well need their old jobs back if the government has a smaller majority at the next election. They have kept up their connections, then, for reasons both of money today and of security in the future. The easiest way these days to determine members' interests outside Parliament is to consult the register kept in the Committee Office of the House, in which such interests are listed and constantly updated. Such a register was called for in the 1950s and 1960s but it was not until the 1970s, in the wake of the Poulson scandal, that it was properly established. Peter Richards, for example, was claiming in 1963 that the 'grey zone' of members' business interests should be made public in a 'return listing any business, trade union or other associations from which they receive payments'.[11] In 1965, James Callaghan, then Labour Chancellor, sneered at Tory members who were opposing his Finance Bill, 'I do not think of them as the member for x, y, or z; I look at them and say "investment trusts", "capital speculation" or "that is the fellow who is the stock exchange man who makes a profit on gilt edge". I have almost forgotten their constituencies, but I shall never forget their interests. I wonder sometimes who they represent, the constituency or their friends' particular interests?' As Roth reports, this was considered at the time to be a breach of parliamentary privilege, for which Mr Callaghan 'half-apologised'.[12] Unpopular as such views might be in the House, the revelations of the Poulson affair, which showed MPs accepting money and favours, meant that the House moved quickly to remove what the Attorney-General then called the 'smoke of suspicion which surrounds the fire of real or imagined corruption'.[13] MPs wanted to establish their credentials with the public, a desire reflected in James Prior's *cri de coeur*, 'We are not crooks and we want it to be seen that we are not crooks.' [14]

Opposition to the registering of interests came from those, such as Enoch Powell, who saw it as an intrusion into members' privacy as well as a slur on their honesty. MPs, so this argument goes, do not need to be treated like untrustworthy children, without discretion or propriety. Yet the Poulson affair showed the vulnerability of members, such as Reginald Maudling, who might claim to be innocent of all corruption, yet by their associations appear to bring the House and the profession of politics into disrepute. It was probably true that, as a colleague later claimed, 'Reggie opened doors [for Poulson] but they led nowhere': yet in the public perception this perhaps only compounded the felony. Maudling acquired the good life for no return.[15] Even with the register of members interests, problems remain: MPs like to be at the centre of things, to be consulted and thought important and influential. As Roth says, 'one can legislate for straight corruption . . . but how can one legislate for ego-tripping and stomach-filling . . . ?'[16]

The development of more professional lobbying in the 1970s and 1980s has also somewhat changed the role of the MP. In 1980 *Private Eye* claimed to be in possession of the minutes of a meeting between the Association of Consultant Architects and Anthony Steen MP (Conservative) in which Steen outlined 'the sort of fee an MP would expect . . . for [giving] special care and attention to their problems'. Geoffrey Rhodes MP claimed that he had been offered £12,000 to help persuade British Airways to use Brindisi rather than Rome as their major Italian airport.[17] A political lobbyist, Douglas Smith, is quoted as saying that, when a civil servant refused to see him, he arranged for his 'tame' MPs to draft some twenty written questions which it was the civil servant's job to answer at length. 'He soon got the message', he says. 'You might call that blackmail, I call it a triumph for inspired democracy.'[18] In the end, of course, MPs have themselves to decide how much and what sort of lobbying is acceptable. There is some evidence that saturation campaigns aimed at uncommitted members are not necessarily successful. For example, the 'hard sell' anti-nationalisation campaign of Bristol Channel Ship Repairers, who moored an entertainment boat near the House and flooded Westminster with PR people, was resented by many MPs as crude and unacceptable.[19]

In spite of this reservation on the part of some, however, the 1985 Register of Members' Interests showed more than 100 MPs acting as parliamentary consultants of one kind or another, and a further 20 who were directors of public-relations companies. As lobbying and public relations become more widespread in politics, the effect of this on Westminster mores is bound to be considerable. At least eight MPs, for example, are currently said to run their own public-relations consultancies and offer advice to clients on government affairs.[20] Peter Fry, the Conservative member for Wellingborough, is a director of Political Research and Communications International and lists over 20 clients in the Register of Interests, ranging from Kentucky Fried Chicken to Airbus Industries.

Some consider that publicly registering such interests is enough: others, such as Patrick Cormack, MP for South Staffordshire and himself a PR consultant, think that there is need for a code of practice and that it is improper, even if he had declared an interest, for an MP to speak on a client's behalf in the House. Such disagreements show the unsatisfactory nature of current practice, where the parameters within which MPs operate are not agreed, and which the 1985 report of the Select Committee on Members' Interests did little or nothing to clarify. In such circumstances, it is likely that the lobbyists and PR consultants will continue to seek support among MPs: that is their job, and, as the then President of the Institute of Public Relations, Kevin Traverse-Healy, has said, 'If the Commons doesn't choose to regulate itself, there is not much that we can do about it.'[21]

The Register of Members' Interests, of course, cannot and is not intended to stop corruption. It is simply an earnest of good faith, an assertion on the part of members that their extra-parliamentary involvements are not secret or underhand. As the register itself makes clear, 'the registering of interests is additional to, and in no way a replacement of, the requirement on members to declare interests when they speak in debate' (and this is no longer just a convention but a rule of the House since May 1974). Members are responsible for notifying changes in their registerable interests within four weeks of the change occurring and these amendments are entered weekly in the typescript register kept in the Committee Office. It is possible, therefore, from an analysis of the register, to identify changes in specific members' interests and also in patterns of involvement. For example, during 1985 there was a 10 per cent increase in MPs' business and commercial consultancies: at the beginning of the year, 310 consultancies were registered; by the end of the year there were 342.[22] Among the extra 32 were the consultancies acquired by Conservatives Michael Portillo, to advise both British Airways and a firm of stockbrokers, and Cranley Onslow with Redifussion plc. The great majority of such appointments are to Conservative members, but Ian Wrigglesworth of the SDP was an adviser to Barclay's Bank and Labour's Gwynneth Dunwoody is a director of the family computer firm.

MPs are expected to register their interests under no less than nine heads: directorships; remunerated employment; trades or professions; financial sponsorship; clients (including personal services by the MP); overseas visits (if not paid for by the member or out of public funds); payments from abroad; land or property; shareholdings (declarable if the member, his/her spouse or children has holdings greater than a hundredth of the issued share capital). Some members, from all parts of the House, enter a nil return. Some are scrupulous about registering anything which might be construed as likely to influence them in any way. Thus Edwina Currie acknowledged a 'gift of hosiery from Courtaulds Ltd' and Angela Rumbold 'an atlas from British Airways'.[23] It is worth noting that the women in the House are particularly light on outside involvements. The Labour women, apart from Mrs Dunwoody's directorship mentioned already, and Dame Judith Hart's journalism and lecturing fees, registered almost nothing but trade-union sponsorship (Ann Clwyd, Harriet Harman and Margaret Beckett by the Transport and General Workers' Union; Clare Short by the National Union of Public Employees; Betty Boothroyd by the General and Municipal Workers and Boilermakers Union; and so on). At the other end of the scale, Cecil Parkinson admitted to 11 directorships and Geoffrey Rippon claimed no less than 32, in 30 of which cases he was chairman of the board.

RECREATION

With their outside interests and their parliamentary duties, it might seem unlikely that MPs would have time for anything else. Yet many of them list recreations which themselves give some indications of the kinds of people who do the job.[24] The most common are, perhaps predictably, the things which can be done at any time, without the need for practice or prior commitment – reading, walking, listening to music, watching sport. However, a fair number also claim to play sports, tennis being particularly popular among the Conservative members. For the more energetic, some claim cycling as a relaxation, while Gareth Wardell is a cross-country runner, John Corrie a hang-glider and Kenneth Warren a mountaineer. Most of the Scots, of all parties, play golf, and Robert Hayward is a rugby referee; but perhaps the most believable is Austin Mitchell, who claims to spend his free time 'contemplating exercise'.

Some MPs, however, seem to be as frantically busy in their private as in their public lives. Robert Wareing, for example, spends his time watching soccer, going to concerts and ballet, motoring and travelling abroad. Ann Winterton, who was formerly joint master of the South Staffordshire hunt, rides, skis and plays tennis, as well as going to the theatre, cinema and concerts. Luckily her husband Nicholas is also to be found on the tennis court, when he's not swimming, jogging or playing squash or hockey.

Some MPs clearly prefer the contemplative to the active pastimes. A few, such as Denis Healey and Ted Leadbitter, paint. Ted Heath's musical talents are well known, but he is not the only musician in the Commons; Ivan Lawrence plays the piano and Robert Key is a tenor with the Academy of St Martin's in the Fields. But undoubtedly the most widespread creative talent among members is writing. This is perhaps rather surprising, as it is often said that MPs seldom write good books.[25] They do not, it is claimed, have the time to think great thoughts and, in any case, they are essentially active rather than cerebral creatures. It is perhaps for this reason that Roy Hattersley, himself a not inconsiderable essayist, bemoans the single-mindedness of modern politicians which has precluded their writing sonnets or, like Gladstone, translating Homer, however imperfectly.[26] But great creative masterpieces aside, the literary output of MPs is, as Trevor Smith has shown, at least as high as it ever was.[27] Certainly MPs are writing more books, pamphlets and articles than their predecessors were fifty years ago, and Smith puts this down to the fact that politicians 'are not just mediators between the governors and governed, they are also brokers between thought and action'.[28] In a situation where academics are no longer publicly politically partisan in the style of Cole or Laski, politicians have been forced to write their own texts. Again, Smith argues, the 'career politician', as identified by Anthony King, will want to take on this role as part of the activist politics to which he is committed. About a third of Labour and Conservative MPs are recorded as authors of one kind or another, the majority of these writing on political topics.

Just as literary communication may be an important part of the MP's role, so is the exploitation of the other media – radio and television. MPs need to be known, in their constituencies and on the wider political stage, but they tread a fine line between being given air time as serious people with important messages to convey and being simply acts in the entertainment business. Most MPs are infrequent and unprofessional broadcasters, brought in only occasionally when their constituency or specialism is in the news. A few become media 'personalities', no longer thought of as politicians, but, rather, famous simply for being famous.

Among the more surprising pursuits recorded by MPs must come the poodle-breeding confessed to by Renee Short and the bee-keeping which intrigues Archy Kirkwood; and who would have guessed, if he had not put it in *Dod's*, that Eric Heffer's favourite pastime is reading philosophy? In the non-sexist House, cooking is not just the relaxation of the women members, for, although Anna McCurley and Jill Knight both claim to enjoy it, so does Jack Straw. Robin Cook, perhaps more realistically, gives not cooking but eating as his favourite occupation. And, if there are political differences sometimes to be found between the leisure activities of the different parties, these are not always clear-cut. It is true that there is the expected tendency to hunting, shooting and fishing among some Tories, yet Labour's Stanley Thorne is hardly conforming to the stereotype with his avowed predelictions for bridge and golf. Honour is perhaps retrieved, however, by his colleague William Michie, who states his only interests as darts, football and allotments.

FAMILY LIFE

Almost certainly the most honest members are those, such as James Couchman, who list their main recreation as 'politics'. The job leaves little time for anything else, mentally or physically. Politicians live and breathe politics, and when they are not practising it they are thinking about it. Reading their recreational claims, one often gets the impression that these are the things they would like to do in another life. This is nowhere more evident than when they are talking about their families. Many members – Clare Short, Peter Thurnham and Edwina Currie, to name a few – list family and family life among their recreations. John Patten even enters a touching 'talking to my wife' as his chosen hobby; one can be sure he seldom gets the chance. And yet the people often most demanded of by politicians are their families. Wives hold the constituency fort while their MP spouses are at Westminster all week; children grow up with only a hazy recollection of father. Indeed, it has been claimed that MPs are not really family men at all. 'In generalising their love of humanity they deprive more specific objects like a wife and children of most of it'.[29] Whether this is true or not most of them are deeply conscious of the amount of time they spend away from their families and evince a degree of guilt, particularly where their children are concerned. Alexander Pollock, with a constituency in the north of Scotland, spends Friday night on the sleeper to Glasgow and then takes the 'plane to Inverness, spending Saturday travelling round some of the 700-odd square miles of his constituency. 'I try to keep Sunday for the family', he says, echoing the majority of MPs to whom we talked. Roger Freeman lives in London but has a flat in his constituency, Kettering. It takes the family two hours to drive there, and, although he says he tries to keep Saturday afternoon and Sunday free, he is in the constituency and always likely to be called on. Living in a constituency nearer to Westminster, however, need not be the answer. Andrew Hunter is the member for Basingstoke, to and from which he tries to commute. This means in reality that he's away from home two or three nights a week. At weekends he is largely working in the constituency; 'I try to keep one weekend in five for the family', he says.

The best strategy for the MP who wants to keep in contact with his family is probably to live in London, regardless of the site of the constituency. It is then possible, given the erratic hours of the House, to see children and spouses more or less daily. Tom Sackville, for example, although his constituency is in Bolton, lives in London and is thus able to see his wife and young child in the early evening before he goes back to Westminster. But, in spite of parliamentary allowances, the expense of running two homes is clearly not possible for everyone, and most families have to try to come to terms with the separations: says one Labour wife, 'You get used to it, you find you have to adjust when they come home for the recess.' The travelling-problem is particularly acute if the member feels the need to spend the whole week in London, or at least from Monday to Friday morning. Newly elected members seem particularly prone to believe that, since Westminster is clearly the centre of the world, they will miss something if they leave. More experienced players of the game have often learned to make time for home and have modified their habits accordingly. Dennis Canavan, for example, has travel to his Scottish constituency down to a fine art. By car either end and 'plane, it takes three hours or so. He says he used to be at Westminster until the shop shut, but after many years (he was elected first in 1974) he has changed his habits and now comes to London on Tuesdays and goes back on Thursday evenings. Far from detracting from his ability to do the job, he believes, it enhances it and his personal life.

For women members there are added problems. On top of the travelling, they may feel the responsibility of keeping the family together and supporting husbands as they themselves need to be supported in their work. Most women come to the Commons either childless (like Lynda Chalker, Janet Fookes or Marjorie Mowlem) or when their children are grown up (like Elisabeth Peacock or Audrey Wise). Some send children to boarding school (Ann Winterton, Edwina Currie) and a few struggle through with nannies and au pairs (like Harriet Harman, Ann Taylor and Virginia Bottomley). But in all cases the tensions between job and family can be great. The single-mindedness demanded of the politician does not fit easily with the socially-accepted roles of supportive wife and mother and it may only be realistically possible to combine the two if children are older or if the member's constituency is in or near London. Then he/she may sometimes be able to get home for 'an indulgent evening with the children', like Rosie Barnes in Greenwich. In Hilary Armstrong's view, it is no coincidence that the three women members from the North-East are all single: 'it would be impossible to do the job with family commitments.'

The children of MPs have much to put up with and many of them are clearly aware of their deprivation in later life.[30] Members are, however, at least aware of their obligations here. When asked about reforms of the House which they might support, several of the Scots members thought changing the dates of the summer recess to coincide with the (rather earlier) Scottish school holidays was at least as important as extending the ten-minute rule or having a fixed parliamentary timetable. And, as children get older, the problem simply becomes more complicated. One wife told of her husband's surprise the first time the children all had other activities planned on the afternoon he had dedicated to the family. 'He was quite shocked,' she says, 'especially when our daughter told him he couldn't expect them to be free just because he had ten minutes to give them!'

If children are not always understanding, or forgiving, spouses are meant to be, and in over 90 per cent of cases 'spouses' means wives. Most wives are involved in the job in some way, and only a small proportion (under 15 per cent) claim to have an independent life, with their own job and interests. At the other end of the scale are the secretary wives, who either run an office in the constituency or answer mail and phone from home, paid from their husbands' secretarial allowance. The wives of Mark Fisher, Stuart Bell and Archy Kirkwood perform this kind of role and, in effect, look after the constituency when their husbands are in London. The advantages of this system are not only practical, but, as Archy Kirkwood shrewdly points out, 'It keeps you together, gives you some life in common. . . .' Most wives, however, are not so fully involved in the family business. They help out as best they can, answering phones, fielding constituents' problems and keeping the show on the road; but the life for most is lonely and difficult to plan. In similar vein, the husband of a Conservative woman member says, 'The worst thing is not knowing how her diary will change with almost no notice. We have to fight for an evening together and sometimes these will be sabotaged by the whips.' Spouses are occasionally to be seen at Westminster having a drink or a meal with the member, or waiting hopefully in the Family Room, the House's one concession to family life. The only answer seems to be that found by the members who write their families into their diaries, who self-consciously set aside time which was sacrosanct, so that, as one put it, 'the whips can whistle . . . the family need me more'. For most, however, the family is far away, the whips are ever-present and personal relationships the losers to the job.

NOTES

1. *Review Body on Top Salaries: Report no. 20, Review of Parliamentary Pay and Allowance*, Cmnd 8881 (1873) II, table 4, p.13.
2. See D. Searing, 'The Role of the Good Constituency Member and the Practice of Representation in Great Britain', *Journal of Politics*, 47 (1985) 374–7.
3. Ibid., pp. 349–50.
4. *HC Deb.*, vol. 739, cols 60–1, 1966.
5. *HC Deb.*, vol. 90, cols 1058–9, 29 Jan. 1986.
6. See Searing, in *Journal of Politics*, 47, p. 358; P. Richards, *The Backbenchers* (Faber and Faber, 1972) pp. 166–7; and A. Barker and M.

Rush, *The Member of Parliament and his Information* (Allen and Unwin, 1970) pp. 194–6.

7. A. King, *British Members of Parliament: A Self-Portrait* (Macmillan for Granada TV, 1974) p. 39.
8. *Review Body of Top Salaries: Report no. 20*, II, table 5, p. 14.
9. C. Mellors, *The British Member of Parliament: A Socio-Economic Survey* (Saxon House, 1978) p. 86.
10. M. Burch and M. Moran, 'The Changing British Political Elite, 1945–83: MPs and Cabinet Ministers', *Parliamentary Affairs*, 38, no. 1 (1985) 14.
11. P. G. Richards, *Honourable Members*, 2nd edn (Faber and Faber, 1963) p. 198.
12. A. Roth, *The Business Background of MPs* (Parliamentary Profiles, 1981) p.xxv.
13. *HC Deb.*, 874, col. 528, 22 May 1974.
14. Ibid., col. 410.
15. Roth, *The Business Background of MPs*, p. ix.
16. Ibid., p. x.
17. A. Doig, *Corruption and Misconduct in Contemporary British Politics* (Penguin, 1984) p. 199.
18. Roth, *The Business Background of MPs*, pp. iii–iv.
19. Doig, *Corruption and Misconduct*, p. 213.
20. A. Raphael, 'MPs Prepared Fudge on Cash Sweeteners', *Observer*, 1 Dec 1985.
21. Quoted ibid.
22. See *The Times*, 28 Dec 1985.
23. All the following examples are taken from the Register of Members' Interests for the week of 17 Feb 1986.
24. These are to be found in, for example, *Who's Who* and *Dod's Parliamentary Companion* (see the 1986 edns).
25. On some of the reasons for this, see B. Pimlott, 'How to Middle through', *Guardian*, 19 Sep 1985.
26. *Guardian*, 1 March 1986.
27. T. A. Smith, 'Men of Affairs as Men of Letters', paper presented to the Annual Conference of the Political Studies Association, Apr 1983.
28. Ibid., p. 2.
29. A. Mitchell, *Westminster Man: A Tribal Anthropology of the Commons People* (Methuen, 1982) p. 239.
30. Ibid., pp. 239–40.

7

Backbench Views of the Job

> *MPs are celebrities in their own constituencies, well known, respected, asked for their opinion, indeed the voice of government. And yet on their return to Westminster, they are once again only minnows, one of the 500-odd backbenchers with no special status or rights other than to be lobby-fodder for their party.*
>
> (Alexander Pollock MP)

The job in Parliament has always had a certain fascination both for those at Westminster and for those who aspire to join them. Perceptions of what the job entails have been varied, though no modern member, one hopes, has such a crude view of it as Anthony Henry, who in 1714, when asked by his constituents to vote against the budget, declared,

> Gentlemen. I have received your letter about the excise and I am surprised at your insolence at writing to me at all.
>
> You know, and I know that I bought this constituency. You know and I know that I am determined to sell it; and you know what you think I don't know, that you are now looking out for another buyer; and I know what you personally don't know, that I have found another constituency to buy.
>
> About what you said about the excise: may God's curse alight upon you all, and may it make your homes as open and as free to the excise officers as your wives and daughters have always been to me while I represented your rascally constituency.[1]

Anthony Trollope, an unsuccessful aspirant, saw the job as something more rewarding: 'I have always thought that to sit in the

126

British parliament should be the highest object and ambition of every educated Englishman.'[2]

Once in Parliament, backbench members often experience anger, frustration and boredom. They also find the job fascinating and rewarding. On the one hand, Woodrow Wyatt expressed a common viewpoint when he wrote that 'the backbench MP performs a trivial function, however interesting it may be'.[3] On the other, Nigel Nicolson, who lost his constituency over his position on Suez, insisted,

> Parliament is not dull. How can it be dull when almost every facet of the nation's life and work comes up sooner or later for debate and where daily a Member associates with men who have immense power in their hands? ... it is not so much boredom which robs him of his early enthusiasm as unfulfilled ambition or laziness.[4]

Paul Rose, who also resigned his seat, saw it differently again:

> All too often the backbencher feels he is a small and not too important cog in an impersonal machine. He sees his function as lobbyfodder at Westminster and as a public relations and welfare officer in his constituency. He sees the government consulting industrialists, trade unionists and economists over prices and incomes before asking the opinions of their backbenchers.[5]

And he went on to state, 'the increasing power of the executive and the bureaucracy that so often run government departments is rapidly devaluing the role of the individual member'.[6]

Clearly much will depend on expectations and how backbenchers decide to channel their energies and accept the limitations of power. There are those who find it difficult to get over their early disenchantment. One well-known commentator has noted,

> The parliamentary glitter fades all too quickly for the backbench Member. He discovers that the accommodation provided for him is not overgenerous. He finds that hardly anyone knows who he is, and even fewer care; his majority is better known than is his name and the whips are more interested in his vote than in his voice.[7]

This view, however, is balanced by the feeling of newcomers that they have won a ringside seat at the centre of power, and this, for a time, may enable them to put up with the frustrations of the job:

> It's the endless fascination of having a front row seat in the stalls at the most interesting of all theatrical performances. One does feel, or I feel, that one is pretty close to the centre of the stage on the major affairs of the country.[8]

Or, as one MP has admitted,

> The chores are all there; the frustrations are all there; but the opportunities are all there too. Because it offers these opportunities, I find it a wider, more exciting thing than any profession I've been in.[9]

And, despite the general complaints, a considerable number would agree with the following statement:

> I do have to admit that there is, very occasionally, a moment of reward, when you achieve perhaps a very small thing – to do with a pensioner or something like that. Those moments really make up for an awful lot of the minuses.[10]

One Conservative member said that what he enjoyed most about the job was,

> first of all, just being a representative under our system, and all the things that go with that: the people, groups who come and see you and feel that you can be of some use and that you can exert influence in parliament. Then the fact that once a year or so one is able to influence some decision that is being made in government. And, third, I suppose the hope that one day one might be allowed to play with the big boys.[11]

One of the problems, as we have seen, is the lack of a job description. Although constituents see their members of Parliament in somewhat simplistic terms – someone only interested in local issues, who will express voters' concern about national issues, deal with constituents' personal problems and attend meetings in the constituency, backbenchers themselves perceive their jobs as infinitely more complex. Austin Mitchell, one of the shrewdest and funniest commentators on the political scene, has this to say on the subject:

> To be a Member of Parliament is to have a choice among a Job Centre's worth of jobs, all to be performed under the roof of a beautifully laid out parliamentary enterprise zone where anything goes. The workforce is given minimal provision and set free to do what it chooses. A modern MP has to be legislator, lawyer, particularly the barrack-room variety, advocate for a cause, party man, organisation man, committee man, researcher, social worker, local ombudsman, constituency advocate, interpreter of government, orator and thinker, showbiz personality, a father confessor, pressure group lobbyist and lobbied critic and defender, adult education lecturer, mediaman and demagogue. . . . In a specialised and sophisticated system of government he is the jobbing labourer.[12]

But, whatever the boredom and the disillusionment, MPs who lose their seats long to return. In retrospect the job appears fulfilling, delightful even:

> It is a unique job. Your opinion is sought and your views matter, first where the rules of our society are made, and, second, day to day on a range of subjects. You might not be very powerful but you have opportunities for influence not easily gained elsewhere. . . . I found it harder work and longer hours than I had imagined and than I have ever otherwise worked. I also found it deeply satisfying to be able to help people and to have a platform for your own deeply held convictions and to act as a spokesman for your party and your own beliefs.[13]

How far do backbench MPs echo the above sentiments? How have the expectations of the role commonly attributed to them been fulfilled in practice? Our interviews and the All-Party Reform Group questionnaire revealed the diversity of backbench perception of the role of the MP.

We have broken down the replies from these sources under the following heads:

– perception of the job;

– expectations concerning accommodation, workload, influence over national policy, influence over party policy, effectiveness in handling constituency problems;
– job satisfaction.

PERCEPTION OF THE JOB

The All-Party Reform Group questionnaire asked members of Parliament what they considered to be the main job of the backbencher. Ten definitions were suggested:

(1) local ombudsman
(2) spokesman for local interests
(3) contributor to the national debate
(4) specialist
(5) trainee minister
(6) party politician
(7) law-maker
(8) check on the executive
(9) constituency welfare officer
(10) educator, and explainer of government policies.

These were to be listed in order of importance by members.

Despite well-publicised grumbles from a considerable and growing number of backbenchers that the job requires them to be simply a human postbox or an overburdened social worker, the majority of the MPs who answered the questionnaire still saw their main job as contributing to national debate. This was closely followed by speaking for local interests and acting as a check on the executive. There was cross-party agreement that 'trainee minister' was the least important role (no doubt a pragmatic acceptance of the fact that only around one third of backbenchers ever become ministers). The fact that 'specialist' was the second least important role must also reflect the ever more diffuse knowledge needed by MPs.

However, if the figures are analysed by party, the picture looks slightly different. Conservative politicians see their main roles as (1) contributing to national debate, (2) speaking for local interests, (3) checking the executive and (4) acting as an educator and explainer. For Labour politicians the priorities are (1) speaking for local interests), (2) contributing to national debate, (3) acting as a constituency welfare officer and (4) participating in party politics. Centre parties' members provide yet another pattern. They believe that the most important aspect of their job is acting as a check on the executive, and rank next in order of importance contributing to national debate, speaking for local interests and acting as a constituency welfare officer.

Some interesting differences of concern and emphasis emerge from the analysis. For example, whereas checking the executive came third overall, Labour Party backbenchers saw it as less important than other members did, ranking it only sixth. On the other hand, the constituency welfare-officer role, ranked third by Labour members, came seventh among Tories, who placed greater emphasis on the role of educator and explainer than did the other parties, for which it was far more peripheral.

Some of these differences of perceptions probably reflect the special circumstances of the 1983 parliament. Given a Tory majority of 144, Labour members had little real hope of acting as a check on the executive, while reselection has inevitably increased the importance of the constituency role for Labour MPs. The attachment to the role of educator and explainer among Conservatives probably also reflects their greater distancing from constituency problems, as seen in their relatively low regard for the welfare-officer role. Conservative backbenchers often still appear to see themselves as having national rather than local interests, much as they did in the late 1960s.[14]

EXPECTATIONS

We have discussed members' attitudes to their job as legislators, as a check on the executive, as debaters of national issues, and as representatives of their constituents. We also asked members to cast their minds back to the time before they were elected: what had they expected the job to be like? And, after election, how did they come to terms with any differences between their expectations and the reality they encountered?

Expectations about accommodation

The environment in which people work can affect the way in

which they work. Cramped quarters with poor facilities, shared rooms, desks in corridors – this is the environment in which, as we have seen, backbenchers have to live, write letters, read papers and make decisions. Had they expected anything else?

Of those members interviewed, the majority had expected little different. They were fairly realistic, or, as one MP put it, 'I knew it would be lousy; my expectations were fulfilled.' Others had presumed that they would share a room but it had not occurred to them that they might share a corridor. Some had been told that conditions at Westminster were quite ramshackle, and had not expected a palatial suite; on the other hand, as one MP put it, 'I did expect to be allocated a desk and some space.' What appalled him was that it took six weeks even to get this, and in the meantime he and other newly arrived MPs simply squatted where they could. A more cynical view was expressed by one MP who said that he had never had any expectations about accommodation. He had always assumed that the House of Commons was party to the idea that Britain was a nation of amateurs and that he was therefore unlikely to find anything efficient and professional about arrangements at Westminster when he got there.

In general members had not been certain what they would get and were slightly bemused by it all. A few had hoped for better things. Sean Hughes MP, for example, followed Harold Wilson, the ex-Prime Minister, as Labour member for Huyton, and had been accustomed to visiting his predecessor in his impressive office in Westminster. This left him with the impression that all MPs worked in such style and, he recalls, the shock was considerable when he was offered his 'grotty room' to be shared with three others!

Expectations about workload

As we have seen, MPs' workloads have increased. What did the 1980s' intakes expect of that workload?

Not surprisingly, one point was continually stressed: there was no such thing as 'an adequate job description'. There was also general agreement that the workload was far heavier than antici-pated. MPs were always tired; the hours were 'too long and too late' – or, as more than one member said, 'just stupid'.

For others it was the volume of mail, the number of letters and the endless pressure-group circulars, that surprised them. Those in marginal seats said that they could never afford to answer letters with a standard reply, which might have helped. Even if this had been possible, the case work that poured in seemed insurmountable. It all produced an emotional strain which left members exhausted, 'trying to cope while having too much on the mind'. Members saw themselves as floundering in 'shifting quicksand', their heads filled with the problems which spilled out of their filing-cabinet.

Some of those with ten years' experience in the House thought that what was important was not so much that the workload had increased as that the balance had been lost; more and more time was being spent on constituency work to the detriment of other aspects of the job. Cases now seemed more difficult and complex; letters had to be longer. The new Select Committees also took up more time; there were more of them and they too produced more reading-matter.

Others, although acknowledging that the workload was greater than they had anticipated, nevertheless made the point that members could set their own level and standard of work: if they were conscientious and ambitious, obviously the work was heavier, but it was also a question of self-discipline. It was, too, a question of choice which aspect of the job should predominate at any particular time. The problem about constituency cases, however, as many members accepted, was that the increase in volume reflected the realities of a political situation where more people needed more help.

One new MP admitted that he had always expected the workload to be high – he had been well briefed. He knew, as he put it, that he would have to be 'conscientious but not mad'. On the other hand, what had surprised him was what he perceived as the incompetence of the Westminster machine. The word *mañana*, he said, had been 'invented neither in South America nor in Spain, but clearly in Westminster and Whitehall'. It was this inefficiency that he found so frustrating.

If MPs were scarcely surprised by their accommodation, but perhaps expected a rather more manageable workload, to what extent had they felt, before election, that they would be effective?

Expectations about effectiveness and influence

Influence over national policy
Given the large Tory majorities of the 1980s, expectations were

based on this reality. Labour members may have felt unable to influence an apparently invincible government. However, interview answers from opposition members varied. Some stated they had few illusions, for, as one of them put it, 'you realise early on that there is no point in being in the House of Commons unless you are in the government or want to be a backbench MP who uses all his ingenuity to take up specific issues'. Otherwise, he went on, there was no parliamentary role for the backbencher. Parliament was simply a talking-shop.

Some MPs, however, talked more in terms of 'exerting influence' than of 'wielding power'. They had hoped, particularly in committees, to have an effect on legislation. One Labour member said that he still believed it was possible for the backbencher to have some influence, particularly in Standing Committees. If a case were argued effectively there, and noticed by a minister prepared to listen, then some modifications in legislation, even though small, could be achieved. Another member was now less optimistic: he really had believed, he said, that he could make a significant contribution to national policy: all he had to do was 'go out and make a speech and the world would change'. He now thought that he could make speeches for ever, but policy was made elsewhere.

MPs who had previously been local councillors were quite clear-sighted as to the limits of their own effectiveness – and all believed that the chairman of a housing committee or the leader of a council had significantly more power than a backbench MP.

Conservative members were more varied in their replies than their Labour colleagues. Backbenchers were not expected to be able to have much influence on national policy, and, given the large Tory majority, a certain amount of cynicism was not surprising. Conservatives too saw the question in terms of influence rather than power – influence which was on the whole limited to modifying the opinions of those prepared to be influenced. The question of committee influence was raised; and most felt that, if a member were prepared to work hard in committee, then it was possible for him or her to have some impact, provided 'you know where to go and who to see'. Persistence, as several members remarked, told in the end.

But there were those who totally rejected such an interpretation. Outsiders, remarked one MP, believe that there are 'various levers which could be pulled'. But, 'once you reach Westminster, you realise that there are no such things'. Another said that he had never expected to have much influence on national policy and was therefore not surprised to be proved right – particularly when his party was in government. In such a context, he said, 'policy is made by a few ministers'.

The overall impression gained was that some members who had started out with fairly low expectations were sometimes pleasantly surprised when great persistence paid off. On the whole, most presumed that such efforts would fail and were vindicated in this belief once in the House.

Influence over party policy
Each party has weekly meetings where backbenchers and the leadership 'exchange views'. In addition, there are regular meetings of the parties' subject committees. Was there a role here for backbench MPs? Had they expected to play one?

Most members come to Westminster with at least fifteen years' working-experience. This means that a very considerable number bring with them specialist interests, knowledge and skills. How useful a weapon were these skills as a means of influencing the party leadership?

A much clearer picture emerges here than in the case of national policy. There was considerable cross-party agreement that the leadership could be talked to and would listen, although it would not necessarily act on suggestions from those with specialist experience. Knowing whom to speak to and when were the key issues – buttonholing people in corridors and participating in discussions in small policy committees were seen as the most important ways of putting across a point of view. One must work closely with those who make decisions, as one member put it: 'Networks work', claimed another.

However, Tory backbenchers admitted that their influence on party policy was minimal – policy was made at the top and even party committees mattered more in opposition than in government. A Conservative MP summed up the balance of his job as social rather than political: 'more of a parish priest than a politician'.

Effectiveness in handling constituency problems
On the whole, members, as we have seen, were surprised at how much work was generated by constituency problems. Did they assume that the energy expended would produce solutions? Those

MPs whose background had been in local government often pointed to the greater effectiveness of the town hall in such areas, but the majority were pleasantly surprised by the arenas opened to them by virtue of their election to Westminster. Unlike in any other area of the job, reality sometimes overtook expectations here. A considerable number agreed that people did 'run around for an MP', that letters were answered promptly, and that, if a member was, as one put it, 'prepared to use some clout and not be highjacked by bureaucrats', this could be effective. Again, as more than one of them suggested, it was not so much that MPs had power as that others perceived them to have it – which may be why businesses, councils and government departments answer member's letters promptly, often dealing quickly with a constituent's problem that they had treated without urgency before the members' intervention.

'Surprised at the high success rate' is perhaps the best way of describing MPs' feelings about their effectiveness in solving constituents' problems. In some areas, such as housing, MPs have little power, but in others, such as immigration, tax and benefit claims, there is, most say, a reasonable possibility of success. One MP declared that he had optimistically believed that once in the House, he would 'prance on a white horse, charge down the High Street and be the saviour of my constituents'. That, he said soberly, had not happened. Yet neither had he failed totally to give help in most cases. The reality was not completely divorced from the expectations.

On the whole, members' expectations here were realised, which is no doubt one of the main reasons why so many immerse themselves in local problems. Here at least, MPs can feel their contribution is important. The growth of the 'social-welfare' role is probably due, as we have seen, not only to the complexities of modern bureaucratic society and the difficulties people face in an economic recession, but also to the pleasure MPs get from the one aspect of their job in which many of them feel fully effective.

Analysis of the constituency load leads on to the question of whether MPs need to be full-time. Given the increasing workload, how did members feel about this? The answers divided very clearly along party lines. On the whole, Labour MPs felt that they ought and needed to be full-time; Alliance members were less sure that this was necessary, while most Conservatives thought it important to have some interests in the world outside politics.

Those who believed that politics was a full-time occupation did so because they felt, as one said, that 'it has to be, if the job is to be done properly – anyway, an active MP knows what is happening outside Westminster without working outside'. Those who were against such concentration thought that the House needed the diversity of interest and wide experience of part-timers. As one said, 'the longer MPs are at Westminster, the more they are divorced from reality'. And he added, 'there is a genuine need to have some knowledge of working practices'. One member, no doubt with the 1983 election in mind, brought up the question of the insecurity of the parliamentary job. The turnover of MPs was considerable, and 'those in marginal seats might well no longer be here in two years' time'. The need to keep up contacts with interests outside Parliament was not just useful in increasing the experience of the House, but necessary in the longer-term interests of MPs themselves.

General expectations
Apart from constituency and policy problems, other expectations were mentioned and compared with the reality at Westminster. Some members felt that these differed in particular in the extent to which the opposition could effectively oppose. Most agreed that the government got away with more than they had thought possible; there was much less accountability than they had imagined before coming into the House.

The variety of the different jobs performed by an MP was also stressed. 'Each part of the work could be a seven-day-a-week job in itself', was one comment. Each part, therefore, was performed less effectively than it might have been had more time been available.

The long and uneven hours of the House were constantly commented on. Although most members had known about the ten o'clock vote before arriving at Westminster, they often declared that they could not have imagined the tedium of the evening hours, when they were frequently in the House but seldom in the Chamber. Some used this time to tidy up all the jobs left over from the day; others read papers and articles and prepared for the next day; but most found the hours difficult to cope with and hated the dead time between 5 and 9 p.m. 'I thought', said one wistfully, 'that when I was elected I would sit in the Chamber and see famous people and talk and have a splendid time.' None of it happened, he said sadly – expectation and reality almost totally parted company.

In some cases, however, members took strength from the fact that things were not as they had expected. One remarked, for example, that he had found, to his surprise and pleasure, that wisdom was not distilled as you went up the executive ladder. The leadership often had feet of clay, instead of the expected genius. On the whole he had found in Parliament men as ordinary as himself, which gave him hope. There were no insuperable barriers ahead and he could as easily get to the top as anyone else!

Job satisfaction

The All Party Reform Group questionnaire attempted to gauge whether members of Parliament were content with their job. The results pointed to a relatively high satisfaction rate: 63 per cent of all MPs were either 'very' or 'fairly' satisfied, with these responses being more or less evenly distributed among the parties. Alliance MPs had the highest satisfaction rate (70.5 per cent), followed by the Tories (67.7 per cent), with Labour MPs least contented (51.7 per cent). One possible interpretation of these figures is that Alliance MPs were the most surprised and grateful to have been returned, while Labour members were angry and disenchanted about their party's second defeat in a row. But it may also be the case that Alliance members are more committed to the constituency role, which, as we have seen, appears to be the most satisfying for the majority of members.

Looking at job satisfaction in relation to age and length of service, the following picture emerges. The older members were the most satisfied, followed by the youngest. 30–40 year olds, with a 73 per cent satisfaction rate, came third, while the middle-aged (ambitions unfulfilled?) were the least satisfied of all. It is reasonable to suggest that those due for retirement have already come to nurture a romantic view of what they are about to lose, while the young are still caught up in the hope and excitement of the beginning of their parliamentary career.

Analysed by party affiliation, the figures show that the highest rate of satisfaction among Conservatives is found among those with the longest years of service (83.8 per cent); while those who have served for 6–15 years showed markedly less satisfaction (57.9 per cent dissatisfied) – ambition unfulfilled again? But the Labour Party shows an interesting reversal here. 87.5 per cent of those with 6–15 years service were highly satisfied, while over 50 per cent of members first elected in 1983 expressed dissatisfaction – a reflection, perhaps, of the frustration inherent in facing a large Tory majority. Dissatisfaction was also common among new backbench members of the Alliance parties, 75 per cent of whom were dissatisfied.

Members were also asked to comment on what they considered the most satisfactory feature of their job. Despite the fact that contributing to national debate, speaking for local interests and checking the executive were seen as the most *important* aspects of the parliamentary role, members felt that their role as constituency MP was the most *satisfactory*. Clearly, here at least the backbencher could achieve success – and effectiveness brought gratification. Among the commonest reasons offered for that gratification were 'finding a satisfactory outcome to local and constituency prob-lems', 'helping to right injustices and to inform', 'winning an issue', 'getting letters of thanks', or, as one MP put it simply, 'getting Mrs McGinty her tax rebate'. And he also went on to admit that he got satisfaction too from 'getting home on Friday' and 'crumpets in the tea rooms'.

Apart from constituency work, other satisfactory aspects of the job mentioned by MPs included the feeling that backbenchers were instrumental in making the law, the sense of independence in the job, the possibility of becoming a specialist in a particular field as a result of easy access to good information, and the variety of the work. One member was particularly enthusiastic about this last element: 'It's a marvellously stimulating life, no day's the same as another: every day brings new things, problems, new people to meet. I love it!' Another, more cynical, stated that his particular satisfaction lay in 'from time to time exploding the myth that frontbenchers can walk on water'.

There was general consensus over the least satisfactory parts of the job. Members complained about the whipping system, with its tendency to reduce MPs to lobby-fodder; the boredom and frustra-tion of 'waiting for Godot', 'sitting in the Chamber all day and failing to be called' or, as some put it, 'just being here'; the parliamentary timetable – 'illogical and irrelevant legislation taken at all hours'; the difficulty of escaping from the job – 'seven days a week, eighteen hours a day, unremitting and remorseless'; and a 'total inability to plan speaking commitments and family life'. One MP complained with feeling that it was 'very difficult to get a sense of direction unless one's interest is narrow or lies in day-to-day self-publicity', while the earlier cynic spoke of his disappointment at 'finding out that frontbenchers can sometimes walk on water'.

NOTES

1. *Review Body on Top Salaries: Report no. 20, Review of Parliamentary Pay and Allowances*, Cmnd 8881 (1983) II, 149.
2. Ibid., p. 222.
3. Ibid., p. 231.
4. R. R. James, *The House of Commons* (Collins, 1961) pp. 47–8.
5. P. Rose, *Backbencher's Dilemma* (Frederick Muller, 1981) p. 48.
6. Ibid., p. 51.
7. W. Wyatt, *Turn again, Westminster* (André Deutsch, 1973) p. 113.
8. Quoted in A. King, *British Members of Parliament: A Self-Portrait* (Granada, 1974) p. 110.
9. Ibid.
10. Ibid., p. 111.
11. Ibid., p. 113.
12. A. Mitchell, *Westminster Man* (Methuen, 1982) p. 26.
13. N. Nicolson, *People and Parliament* (Weidenfeld and Nicolson, 1958) p. 64.
14. J. Mackintosh (ed.), *People and Parliament* (Saxon House, 1978) p. 12.

8

A Month in the Life of Four Backbenchers

The career politician is a person committed to politics. He regards politics as his vocation, he seeks fulfilment in politics, he sees his future in politics.

(Anthony King)

We have already presented the reader with a hypothetical 'day in the life of' two backbench MPs. Its purpose was to highlight the way in which members of Parliament can be absorbed in the processes of Westminster and how their perceptions of backbench influence and opportunities differ.

That account was based on an imaginary day. This chapter, however, deals with realities – the monthly diaries of four members of Parliament, two Tory (to reflect the large Tory majorities in the 1983 and 1987 Parliaments), one Labour and one Social and Liberal Democratic Party. Of the Conservative members, one has a suburban seat, the other a rural/seaside constituency; the Labour MP represents an inner-London constituency; and the SLD MP is the member for a far-flung constituency just north of the Scottish border. Their diaries go some way to answering questions often raised about the nature of the job of a backbencher. Legislator, critic of the executive, party supporter, constituency welfare officer – these are the roles, as we have seen, which members of Parliament perceive themselves as performing. To what extent do the monthly diaries of our four MPs reflect those roles? And does an examination of their work, both in Parliament and in the constituency, highlight any particular pattern that is common to all, irrespective of party?

Outlines given are of the MPs' diaries for the first and third weeks of February 1985. February was chosen as it was the only full month in the 1984–5 session when MPs were in Westminster.

141

ARCHY KIRKWOOD

Archy Kirkwood is the MP for Roxburgh and Berwickshire, which he holds for the Social and Liberal Democrats. He was formerly a solicitor and personal aide to David Steel. He shares a room at Westminster, but has no office or agent in the constituency. His wife, formerly secretary of the Young Liberals, is very politically active and aware, and sees to all his secretarial requirements for both the constituency and the House. He has an assistant in the constituency and a computer at Westminster. In London he lives in a small flat within walking distance of Parliament.

Archy Kirkwood estimates that he works a 90-hour week, spending at least an hour a day, seven days a week, on his mail, of which one third comes from pressure groups, one third is from constituents and one third concerns his specialisms (he is on three party panels – Social Security, Health and Social Services – and is a party spokesman on taxation and social services). He clears much of his correspondence by 'phone, and also finds this the most effective way of carrying out case-work.

He goes into the Chamber for Question Time and tries to hear all questions, because he sees this as 'learning the business'. Because of the small number of SLD MPs, he finds he gets more chance than his Labour or Conservative counterparts to speak in the Chamber. Time spent on committees he reckons at between six and seven hours a week, and party committees and meetings also take up a fair amount of time.

One of the most tiring aspects of his week is the travel. He flies up to the constituency on Thursday night or Friday and takes a sleeper back on Sunday. Owing to this and the great distances he has to cover in his constituency, he estimates that he spends at least ten hours a week travelling. He tries to keep Sunday for his family. Below is an outline of his diary for the first and third weeks of February 1985. He did not have a propitious start to the month!

Diary, February 1985

Monday 4th to Thursday 7th. Ill in bed owing to overwork previous week and a 12-hour tour within the constituency on Sunday. (Wife represented Kirkwood at constituency-party AGM on Wednesday 6th).

Friday 8th. Constituency engagements. Met accountant over local tax problems. 4 p.m., meeting in Hawick: 6.30 p.m., Duns (35 miles away); discussion over limited lists for rural doctors. 7.30 p.m., Duns: local branch meeting. 11 p.m., home.

Saturday 9th. 9.30 a.m., constituency surgery in Roxburgh. 2 p.m., surgery in Coldstream. 7 p.m., evening drinks party for new business venture.

Sunday 10th. Clear.

Monday 18th. Travel to House. 2 p.m., meeting with Atlantic Group of young politicians. 4 p.m., mail.

Tuesday 19th. 9 a.m., mail. 11 a.m., Staffing Committee meeting: discussion on salary structure for staff. 5 p.m., meeting on pesticides (all-party meeting). 7.30 p.m., dinner with constituents.

Wednesday 20th. 9 a.m., mail. 1 p.m., lunch with British Council. 3 p.m., Chamber. 6 p.m., weekly party meeting. 7.30 p.m., dinner with Liberal colleagues and discussion.

Thursday 20th. 10 a.m., meeting with David Steel. 12.30 p.m., lunch: discussion on Scottish Ecumenical Committee meeting. 3 p.m., Treasury Questions. Home to constituency early to attend rural school meeting.

Friday 22nd. 10 a.m., meeting in Hawick with computer experts. 1 p.m., Roxburgh District Officer's lunch. 3 p.m., touring jute factories (40 miles away). 8 p.m., home.

Saturday 23rd. 9.30 a.m.–12.30 p.m., surgery in Roxburgh. 2–4 p.m., surgery in Coldstream.

Sunday 24th. Clear.

ANGELA RUMBOLD

Angela Rumbold is Conservative MP for Mitcham and Morden, in outer London. She was elected to Kingston Borough Council in 1974 and became chairman of the Education Committee. She is a former member of the Burnham Management Committee and Assessment of Performers Unit for the Department of Education.

Angela Rumbold shares a room at Westminster. She has a full-time parliamentary secretary and a constituency secretary. She usually commutes to Westminster from her home in Surbiton, but also has a flat in central London. Now a minister, when interviewed she was Parliamentary Private Secretary to the Secretary of State for Transport.

She estimates her workload at over 80 hours a week. Three hours a day, six days a week, are spent on mail, with about 40 letters a day to be dealt with. She spends about one hour a day in the Chamber, going in for Question Time and for debates of particular interest to her but not much else. She has been on three Standing Committees in three years and thought she must have spent some 20 hours a week on committee work alone. Party committees took up four to five hours.

Travel to and from the constituency is not a problem, as it takes only about 30 minutes. This means that it is possible for her to fulfil evening engagements in the constituency. Because she lives near Westminster, she makes it a rule to try to see her family during the week as well as at weekends. She often goes home between 6 and 10 p.m., or meets her husband for supper in the House. She also keeps Sunday for the family.

Diary, February 1985

Monday 4th. Left home 9.30 a.m. for 10.30 meeting at Department of Transport on Parliamentary Questions. Lunch in House of Commons. 2.30 p.m., Parliamentary Question Time with Secretary of State. 5 p.m., meeting in House of Commons with Transport backbenchers. 7 p.m., left for Mitcham Ward AGM in Fegges Marsh. 10 p.m., back at House for vote. 10.30 p.m., left for home.

Tuesday 5th. Morning on post. 12.45 p.m., lunch meeting with constituency firm. 2.30 p.m., in House for Education Questions. 5 p.m., Aviation Committee backbench. 6 p.m., meeting with Secretary of State and backbenchers. 6.15 p.m., reception in House. 10 p.m., vote. 10.30 p.m., left for home.

Wednesday 6th. 9.30 a.m., meeting in London at Department of Transport. 10.30 a.m., Institute of Statistics lecture. 2.30 p.m., meeting with National Union of Students. 5.30 p.m., meeting in House with constituent. 6 p.m., meeting with Home Secretary. Dinner at House. Home 11.30 p.m.

Thursday 7th. 8.45 a.m., Department of Transport meeting. 10.30 a.m., hair appointment. 12.30 p.m., CBI lunch, House of Commons. 4.15 p.m., Transport Committee. 5.15 p.m., Transport discussion group. Late vote. Home midnight.

Friday 8th. 11 a.m., visit to local industry and lunch. 4 p.m., Advice Bureau. 8 p.m., St Helier Ward AGM. Home at 10 p.m.

Saturday 9th. 9.30 a.m.–12.30 p.m., catching up with post.

Sunday 10th. All-day seminar on airports, Carlton Gardens. Home 5.30 p.m.

Monday 18th. 10.30 a.m., meeting with constituent in Mitcham. 12.30 p.m., lunch at Conservative Central Office with National Women's Committee. 3.30 p.m., Second Reading, Transport Bill. 6 p.m., board meeting for business. Vote 10 p.m. Home.

Tuesday 19th. 10 a.m., parliamentary maritime group meeting. 12.30 p.m., lunch at Carlton Club. 2.30 p.m., Parliamentary Questions in House. 5 p.m., Aviation Committee. 7 p.m, sherry party. 7.30 p.m., meeting about buses. 10 p.m., vote. Home.

Wednesday 20th. 9 a.m., meeting at Department of Transport on Parliamentary Questions. 11 a.m., back to House of Commons. 12.45 p.m., lunch with British Dental Association. 6.30 p.m., private dinner engagement close to House. 10 p.m., vote. Home.

Thursday 21st. 9 a.m., meeting at Department of Transport. 10.30 a.m., Transport Bill Committee. 1 p.m., lunch. 6.30 p.m., Granada TV programme. 10 p.m., vote. Home.

Friday 22nd. Morning on post. 3.30 p.m., Advice Bureau in constituency. 8.30 p.m., meeting with constituents. Home 10.30 p.m.

Saturday 23rd. From 10.30 a.m., meetings in constituency with three different constituents. 12 noon, National Advisory Committee on Education meeting at Conservative Central Office (all afternoon). Home 5 p.m.

Sunday 24th. Clear.

CHARLES WARDLE

Charles Wardle is Conservative MP for Bexhill and Battle, in Sussex. He used to be chief executive of a public company and a member of the CBI Central Council, the CBI West Midlands Council (chairing its Advisory Committee), the Midlands Committee of the Institute of Directors, and the Economic and Finance Committee of the Engineering Employers' Federation. He gave up all these positions on becoming parliamentary private secretary to Norman Fowler, Secretary of State for Health and Social Services, as he knew he would not otherwise have enough time for his parliamentary duties. Charles Wardle believes, unlike many other new MPs, that accommodation in the House is not inadequate. For him, offices do not matter as much as the opportunity for new members to get about and meet their parliamentary colleagues. He has his own secretary, whom he brought with him when he came into the House from industry, makes use of the Conservative offices in Bexhill, and has further secretarial help, when necessary, from his agent's secretary. He has a flat in London, a flat in Gloucestershire near his daughter's school, and a rented home in Battle.

He works in the House all day Monday and on Tuesday, Wednesday and Thursday from lunchtime onwards. Fridays are spent in the constituency and Sunday is family day. He has about 150 letters a week, 100 of which need a reply. His method of dealing with his correspondence is interesting; he dictates letters on the phone and posts others to either his wife or his secretary. Either he or his wife meets his secretary twice a month – sometimes even on the motorway, which is only half an hour from either flat! Charles Wardle spends a considerable amount of time on DHSS work – meeting officials, attending committees and talking to backbenchers. He always attends Health and Social Services Questions and debates in the same area. In addition, he usually attends Prime Minister's Question Time. For other questions and debates, his criterion for attendance is that they should be of general interest or relevant to constituents' concerns.

Diary, February 1985

Monday 4th. 12 noon, meeting with Secretary of State. 1 p.m., lunch with Secretary of State. Afternoon, House of Commons. 7.30 p.m., dinner with chairman of major food company and other Conservative MPs.

Tuesday 5th. Morning, private business. 4.30 p.m., backbench committee meeting. 5.00 p.m., backbench committee meeting. 6 p.m., drinks with Lord Privy Seal.

Wednesday 6th. Morning, constituency mail. Afternoon, House of Commons. 6.30 p.m., meeting with Chancellor of the Exchequer. 7.30 p.m., dinner at House of Commons with industrialists.

Thursday 7th. Morning, private business. Lunch, CBI. Afternoon, House of Commons. 6 p.m, 1922 Committee. Evening paired.

Friday 8th. Morning, House of Commons. 12 noon, left for constituency. 2.30 p.m. and 3.30 p.m., branch AGMs (constituency party). Evening, social engagement in constituency.

Saturday 9th and Sunday 10th. Private family weekend engagement.

Monday 18th. 12 noon, meeting with Secretary of State. Lunch, meeting with Secretary of State. Afternoon and evening, House of Commons, constituency mail.

Tuesday 19th. 11.30 a.m., constituents on guided tour of Palace of Westminster. 1 p.m., private business lunch. 4.30 p.m., backbench committee. 6 p.m., meeting with Secretary of State. 7 p.m., reception at House of Commons. 7.30 p.m., dinner for small company representatives with other Conservative MPs.

Wednesday 20th. Morning, private business. 4 p.m., meeting with investment banker. 5 p.m., meeting with Society of Motor Manufacturers and Traders. 7.30 p.m., dinner with British Airports representatives.

Thursday 22nd. Paired – private family engagement.

Friday 22nd. 2.30 p.m., branch AGM (constituency party). 5 p.m., meeting at constituency Conservative Association headquarters. 7.30 p.m., social engagement in constituency.

Saturday 23rd. 10 a.m., meeting with constituents. 11 a.m., branch AGM (constituency party). 12.30, branch lunch.

Sunday 24th. No engagements.

CHRIS SMITH

Chris Smith is Labour MP for Islington South and Finsbury, in inner London. A former housing-development worker, he was a member of the Islington Borough Council from 1978 to 1983 (Chief Whip 1978–9, Chairman of Housing 1981–3). He is a member of the Council for National Parks. Chris Smith shares a large office with another MP. It is in Norman Shaw North and therefore some distance from the Chamber, which can be inconvenient. He has a secretary and a research assistant (unpaid), but no office in the constituency. He lived in his constituency prior to becoming an MP and has kept his home there.

He thought he had about 250 letters (three hours' work per day) a week, a large chunk of which 'fell into the bin'. Constituency letters came to over 20 a day, and quite a number of his constituents rang the House of Commons. His private telephone number was also well known, as previously he had been Chairman of Housing.

He usually attends Prime Minister's Question Time, and, in particular, questions and debates on the environment, housing, civil liberties and London. He is on the Environmental Select Committee, which takes up a considerable amount of time in meetings (one full meeting each week), visits and reading of research papers. He is also on the Labour Party's Housing and Foreign Policy Committees and at least four to five hours a week are spent on drafting statements for these. He is on the executive of the London Labour Party and the Housing Group.

A fair amount of time is spent travelling backwards and forwards between the constituency and Westminster. Chris Smith tries to shut off on Sundays but finds it very difficult, particularly as his majority is so slim, and sometimes he goes canvassing on Sunday mornings. Being a bachelor, he has no family ties.

Diary, February 1985

Monday 4th. Morning, brief visit to Ponting trial proceedings at Old Bailey; rest of morning working on correspondence. 4.15 p.m., Environmental Select Committee, witnesses from Sports Council. 6 p.m., London Labour MPs Group. 7.30 p.m., Police Consultative Committee at Islington Town Hall. 10 p.m., back at Westminster, vote on coal-industry motion.

Tuesday 5th. 11 a.m., visit to Tavistock Square DHSS office. 3.15 p.m., asked oral questions of Prime Minister. 4–9 p.m., Film Bill report stage (had been on Standing Committee); spoke and intervened on a number of occasions. 7 p.m., London Labour Group, meeting with Inner London Education Authority. 9 p.m., joined other new Labour members for dinner and discussion.

Wednesday 6th. Morning working on correspondence. 2.30–3.30 p.m., Environment Questions; asked about Wildlife and Countryside Bill. 4.15 p.m., Environmental Select Committee, witnesses from Sports Council. 7.30 p.m., visit to new Lesbian and Gay Centre in constituency. 9.30 p.m., voted on Rates Order. 9.50 p.m., Thornhill Ward Labour Party meeting in constituency, then to pub with ward members!

Thursday 7th. 10.30 a.m. to 6 p.m., visit to NIREX and UK Atomic Energy Authority (Harwell) with Select Committee – discussions, inspection of nuclear waste, lunch, etc. 6 p.m., meeting with *Times* journalists on conservation issues. 8 p.m., Barnsbury Ward Labour Party meeting in constituency. 10 p.m., vote on water rates. Sat in on London Transport debate afterwards. After midnight, voted. Home 1 a.m.

Friday 8th. Morning, Second Reading of Wildlife and Countryside

Amendment Bill (spoke). 12 noon, brief appearance at press conference to launch Greater London Council report on private-sector rented housing. 2–5.30 p.m., writing press releases for local press, working on correspondence. 6.30–9.30 p.m., surgery in constituency.

Saturday 9th. 9 a.m. to 1 p.m., constituency-party bric-à-brac fair and a ward party jumble sale. Most of rest of day free!

Sunday 10th. Catching up on correspondence.

Monday 18th. 9 a.m., meeting to shortlist applicants for job of assistant with chair of constituency party and present assistant. 1 p.m., lunch and return to House. 3.30 p.m., debate on Ponting and Belgrano (spoke). 8 p.m., from House to opening of Polytechnic of North London exhibition on work training. 8.30 p.m., speech on rate-capping at public meeting in Islington. 9 p.m., back to House for wind-up speeches on Ponting and Belgrano. Voted at 10 p.m. 10.30 p.m., interview for TV AM. 11 p.m., interview for Independent Radio News.

Tuesday 19th. 10 a.m., accountant (meeting to discuss 1983–4 tax returns). 11 a.m., meeting with Tribune Group assistant (Smith is a secretary of Tribune). 12 noon, correspondence. 3.50 p.m., voted on ten-minute-rule Bill (Coal Industry). 4.15 p.m., Tribune Group meeting. 5.15 p.m., meeting with Campaign for Homes in Central London. 6 p.m., vigil outside South Africa House. 7 p.m., Esperanto group – brief appearance. 7.30 p.m., meeting and dinner with colleagues in Parliamentary Labour Party. 10 p.m., voted on London Road Transport Bill.

Wednesday 20th. 10.30 a.m., Select Committee, then correspondence. 2.30 p.m., Foreign Office Questions (Smith was called first and asked a question on Guatemala). 3.30–6.30 p.m., debate on timing of London Road Transport Bill (spoke). 5 p.m., meeting with *Sun* journalists. 6.30 p.m., voted on timing of London Road Transport Bill. 7 p.m., Labour Campaign for Criminal Justice AGM; re-elected vice-chair. 7.30 p.m., meeting constituency General Management Committee, Islington; afterwards to pub. 11.15 p.m., back to House and voted on Trustee Savings Banks Bill.

Thursday 21st. Morning, correspondence. 1 p.m., lunch with BBC journalist. 4–9 p.m., interviews with applicants for assistant's job. 9–11 p.m., discussion and decision on applicants. 11.30 p.m., voted on Prevention of Terrorism Act.

Friday 22nd. 11.15 a.m., meeting at Islington Town Hall with Chair of Housing. 12.45 p.m., Islington Chamber of Commerce lunch – Kenneth Baker speaking. 2.30–5.30 p.m., correspondence and press releases for local papers. 6.30–8.30 p.m., surgery. 9 p.m., supper with party members and discussion on environmental issues.

Saturday 23rd. 11 a.m., chaired Socialist Countryside Group conference at County Hall. 1.30 p.m., drove to Cambridge; spoke at election 'school' for Cambridge Labour Party. 5.30 p.m., back to Islington. Meeting of Islington Muslim Association. Evening free.

Sunday 24th. 10.45 a.m., canvassing in Holloway Ward. 12.30 p.m., drove to Birmingham to speak at National Union of Students special conference. Returned early evening.

COMPARISONS

What can be deduced from the above entries? Do we find here the independent MP, the committee man/woman, the ministerial aspirant or the constituency member?

Four points immediately stand out. The first is that all the MPs (whatever their majority) spent a considerable amount of time dealing with constituency matters, whether at surgeries, on local visits or writing letters. Clearly those in or near London see more of their constituents than those with more distant constituencies. But even there the MPs' profile is consistently high. The second element that is discernible is that parliamentarians do not waste their time on attending a wide-ranging number of committees, but tend to concentrate on a few. Even though the parliamentary private secretaries generally go to their relevant departmental meetings and committees, it is interesting to note that they also managed to attend committee meetings connected with earlier interests. The length and lateness of parliamentary hours is also very noticeable, and it is clear that members of Parliament fairly consistently work a six-day week, with only Sundays sometimes free.

However time-consuming the constituency work is, it nevertheless brings its own rewards. All four MPs believed that, at least at this level, they could be effective, and therefore found it one of the most pleasurable aspects of their work. MPs should be in close touch with their constituents and ought to be prepared to play a pastoral role – people needed MPs to 'use them as safety-valves'. One of the MPs made the distinction between his role in the constituency and his role in Parliament. In the constituency, he said, he was confident that he knew what he was doing and he could use his power to achieve his ends. However, the general consensus was that constituency work was self-generating. 'You encourage people to 'phone and they do.' 'If you don't want to generate work then you don't have to. But, if you are a good constituency member, people contact you, and this creates more work. If you sit on committees and get informed, you get asked to sit on more committees and so on.' Asked about effectiveness on behalf of constituents, one of the MPs stated, 'I can do more than I dared to imagine, which is very gratifying.'

The nearer the constituency is to Westminster, the more the member is at the beck and call of his or her constituency party. In the first week of February, Chris Smith made on average one visit a day to the constituency on local affairs. The demands made on Angela Rumbold reflect the fact that her constituency is slightly further from the House. On three occasions during the two weeks in question, she spent part of the day working in the constituency, each time on Friday or Monday, when she might have been expected to be there for the weekend anyway. Both MPs have relatively marginal seats. Charles Wardle, with a safe seat in Bexhill, returned to his constituency only at weekends. Archy Kirkwood, also in a marginal, and representing a wide rural area, filled much of his weekend with constituency work, but not surprisingly, given the distance, remained at Westminster during the week.

We can see how the pattern of committee meetings reflects the interests and particular specialisms of the MPs concerned, as well as their duties (in the case of the Conservative members) as parliamentary private secretaries. Interests are varied. Chris Smith, with a background of involvement in environmental issues, attended Environmental Select Committee sessions and spoke in environment-related debates, as well as participating in debates on London and other issues and concerning himself with the trial of Clive Ponting, a constituent of his. Archy Kirkwood's activities reflect the nature of SLD parliamentary politics: with so few MPs, he is a member of three party panels, three in different areas all needing different skills, as well as being a party spokesman and dealing with Scottish affairs. Angela Rumbold, as a parliamentary private secretary in transport, nevertheless kept up her previous interests by attending Education Question Time and seeing members of the National Union of Students and National Advisory Committee on Education, of which she used to be chairman. Charles Wardle, as we can see from his meetings with industrialists and the CBI, maintained his contacts with industry.

The four MPs were most alike in their pattern of attendance at debates and Question Times. Only those debates (and those were few in number) which held a particular interest were attended, and the same generally applied to Question Times. In all four cases, attendance was most regular at debates or questions concerned with the MPs' special areas of responsibility in the party and Parliament.

And what of private business? Angela Rumbold took half an hour off to have her hair done; all the MPs had most of Sunday off; Charles Wardle managed to keep some weekday evenings free, Chris Smith didn't. Archy Kirkwood travelled and travelled.

The heavy workload and the long and late hours stand out. We asked the MPs how they had reacted to their six-day week when they came into the House. Most agreed that they had thought the workload would be lighter, that, as Chris Smith said, 'people wouldn't come with their housing problems'. He went on to say that he couldn't write a standard letter to anyone, because of his low majority. The number of meetings also appalled him – he never had time either to sit at his desk or to think. Charles Wardle believed it was not so much a question of too much work (more manageable than many supposed) but that some MPs were inexperienced at dealing with administrative work and that it was the personal inefficiency of such members that brought pressure on themselves.

Angela Rumbold was also surprised at the workload, but admitted that a good deal of work was to some extent generated by MPs themselves. If constituents were encouraged and letters were replied to efficiently, then this immediately generated more work. But in general she found that the job 'vastly exceeded my expectations in terms of job satisfaction and what I can do'. Archy Kirkwood saw the job as 'a treadmill you can't get off'. Yet he said that he felt he could do things for people more effectively than he had imagined, but that this required a lot of effort and a lot of time. The hours were worse than he had thought: 'it's a total take-over of your life'. Again he stressed how the work was self-generating. 'You encourage people to 'phone and they do. You make work for yourself, but in a marginal constituency I feel I have to do this.'

The diaries reflect a common preoccupation. All four members of Parliament belong to that well-known breed of politician – the self-generating workaholic. However, is all the perpetual motion simply an end in itself – reflecting members' vested interest in looking busy and making the job appear difficult? Is the job as substantial as it looks? Does the backbencher ever address central issues – for instance, important policy questions? Is there a sense of purpose? Are there clearly defined objectives and priorities?

The diaries reflect our earlier conclusions. Members of Parliament are preoccupied with endless meetings, ceaseless letters, difficult constituency problems. Despite their criticism of its value (see Chapter 9), they attend Question Time more frequently than debates. Their lives are no longer centred round the Chamber – if, indeed, they ever were. There is the sense of an 'endless treadmill' of late nights and early mornings, perhaps allowing little time for reflection. Work for the sake of work?

9

Changes

Parliament as presently constituted is a sick joke. If something is not done to improve the way it is run, I will either spend far more time in my constituency ... or pack the whole thing in and earn an honest living elsewhere.

(SLD MP)

This book has given a descriptive rather than a prescriptive account of the job of a backbencher, based on what members have said in response to surveys and interviews with the authors and others. The jobs done and the priorities within them have varied widely. What changes members advocate depend on what view they take of their job and more broadly, though perhaps less consciously, of the role of Parliament itself.

There are members who, given the recent years of large majorities and strong government leadership, claim that Parliament is acting now merely as a rubber stamp for government legislation, 'but stamping so lightly as to be almost illegible'.[1] Indeed, nearly all legislation passed, as we have seen, is either initiated or supported by the government and as the TSRB report[2] acknowledges, 'few backbenchers seem to expect significantly to influence government legislation once it is before the House.' Yet opportunities of doing so *before* it gets to the House are also limited, despite members' assertion that influence rather than power is their strong suit. Where there are large government majorities tamed by the Whips and more and more PPS jobs driving the numbers actively involved in the government up to over 130 members, observers inside Parliament and outside it worry that Parliamentary sovereignty itself is declining into mere 'elective dictatorship'. There is some support, therefore, for the idea of a written constitution defining the precise role of Parliament and the limits of government

155

government power which in turn would identify more precisely the role of a backbencher in the legislative and governmental process. On the whole, however, members do not put their complaints about the terms and conditions which go with their hard-won jobs explicitly into the broader context of the role of Parliament, but confine themselves to immediate problems.

The Procedure Committee has defined the principal objective of Parliamentary activity as 'to put the policies and actions of the government under close scrutiny'. Members' suggestions for change reflect considerable doubt that they have the means adequately to fulfil this function. One member, Graham Allen, a leading advocate of reform has put a stark view: 'by almost any practical test, the government escapes effective scrutiny by our elected representatives.'[3]

As one outside commentator has written: 'The House of Commons sits for twice as many hours per year as most Western legislatures. A Rayner-style scrutiny on Parliament would begin by asking whether this enhanced or diminished the quality of its output in terms of an effective monitoring of Government actions or the efficient production of well-drafted legislation.'[4]

The All Party Reform Group highlighted members' dissatisfactions with the conditions under which they work. Many do not necessarily like the way the system is run, they often resent the pay, poor accommodation and inadequate back-up service, and conscientious, hard-working members are exhausted by the long and late hours. Interest in reform is, however, as one MP has put it, a minority sport. For politicians, he accepted, 'keeping their heads above water is more absorbing than thinking about the why and the how of the job'. Members respond to the immediate problems of shortage of time, of the pressures and frustrations produced by the demands of Commons and constituency combined. The evidence is that these demands are growing, so that Parliament, from the parliamentarians' point of view, is in danger of becoming what one characterised as 'a legislative factory, manned by harassed, over-worked MPs' with too little time left to think out their primary roles and to plan their strategies accordingly. MPs are 'condemned to dash like disorganised firemen from crisis to crisis to crisis, always arriving with a noise and clamour in direct ratio to their tardiness and effectiveness, before moving on to the next pile of dying embers'.[5] Nevertheless, there are aspects of the job which it is increasingly felt could and should be changed.

SALARIES AND ALLOWANCES

Not all MPs believed that parliamentary salaries ought to be higher, but some still argue that, even after the latest reforms, something more ought to be done about pay and allowances. A number of MPs included in our survey believed that salaries should lie somewhere between £25,000 and £30,000. If salaries did not increase, one MP ominously declared, 'the extra money might well have to be made up through the back door' – by allowances, for example. A woman MP thought salaries ought to be trebled and that this would encourage better people to come in perhaps for a shorter time. People should treat being an MP as 'a career move. Give a high salary and expect people to earn it.' She also pointed out that what MPs have at present is 'a high risk contract for four years'. It is, she added, particularly expensive to be a woman MP, having to pay for domestic help and having clothes and hair always looking presentable.

Another member had a more radical solution, suggesting that reform should be 'all or nothing'. Either there should be 'huge increases to pay full-time MPs or there should be no salary at all, and MPs would only come to the House when there was a debate to which they wanted to contribute'. Or, again, as a Conservative member advised, 'Don't stand for parliament unless you have made some money.' This echoed the sentiment of another Tory: 'I sense', said Roger Freeman, 'that a disturbingly large number of my colleagues find the commitments of being a member financially onerous. This is possibly a bit dangerous because they go looking for jobs and are not too choosy about what they take.'

MPs are, however, with some voluble exceptions, reluctant to be demanding in public on better pay and conditions. It is not a popular concern of their constituents, and most of the electorate, as members are only too aware, believe that their representatives are fairly amply rewarded already. Members may be right to tread warily here; it has been claimed by at least one expert that the decline in the prestige of the professions, including that of politics, is at least partly due to the fact that their practitioners 'have all campaigned on their own behalf, seldom for the services in which they work ... [which] is to fail an important test of professional responsibility'.[6]

The question of pay may never really be satisfactorily resolved, it seems, until the full-time/part-time distinction is dealt with. For those who work an 80-hour week, the rate of pay works out at well below the average wage; seen in those terms, the case for a rise looks strong and it is hard to think of any trade union which would not consider its members exploited if they were similarly remunerated. On the other hand, there are clearly those, both in and outside the House, who believe that members should have other involvements, which can be expected to 'top up' the parliamentary stipend. Many, particularly on the Conservative side, believe that the value of the part-time job is not only in providing a variety of experience in the House, but also in allowing those whose earning-capacity is such that they could never be paid comparably for the parliamentary job to take on a political role which they would not otherwise contemplate. Perhaps we do need a sliding scale in salaries, discriminating between those who give all their time to politics, and are therefore available to sit on committees and participate in running the House, and those who are never at Westminster in the mornings. Such a 'points system' might seem crude, but it would deal with the increasing tendency of MPs, particularly Labour and both centre parties, to be full-time and therefore arguably due a better financial return. It would also mean that those who make a different contribution to the work of the House would not be excluded. And, if it is claimed that this would unfairly discriminate against the latter, it can surely be argued that their political connections are often the very reason why their professional advice is sought, and that this, rather than simply their parliamentary salary, brings their financial reward.

One way in which all MPs might be given a pay rise would be by decreasing the number of parliamentary constituencies and therefore representatives. In other words, if we had fewer MPs, we could afford to pay them more. On the face of it, there is no reason, apart from a historical one, why we should have 650 representatives at Westminster, and, indeed, the number has fluctuated since the war, with a low of 625 in 1950 and the present high introduced in 1983.[7] Why should a relatively small geographical area such as Britain need more political representatives than, say, West Germany, where the Bundestag has 520 members, or France, where the Assemblée Nationale has 577, or the vastly larger United States of America, where 435 members of the House of Representatives suffice.[8] However, on all the survey evidence, our own included, MPs themselves are adamantly opposed to cutting their numbers. This might seem, on the face of it, a purely self-interested response. What group, after all, is likely to agree to its own decimation? But the argument made here is not so much about self-protection as about the special relationship which members have with their constituents and the weakening of that tie if they are expected to represent larger areas in a much more impersonal way. Whatever the objective force of this argument, it is clearly backed for most MPs by strong and genuine emotions, which, in view of the important part we have seen constituency representation playing in the job, is perhaps unsurprising. In opposing a cut in their numbers, MPs may not simply be protecting their patch but also rejecting the possibility of weakening what, for many of them, is the most or even only satisfying part of the job.

Whereas the salary is still thought by some to be on the low side, the allowances claimable in terms of travel, secretarial assistance, accommodation, and so on, are generally recognised to be much more generous. In some cases, however, MPs are critical of the way their allowances work out. For example, the car allowance is so structured, some contend, as to encourage members to run a larger car than they may need. Again, many, particularly of the younger MPs, feel that their allowances do not allow them to acquire the support they need to do the job (despite the 1986 TSRB findings: see chapter 5), especially in the constituency. They quickly use up their secretarial allowances at Westminster and, unless they have a rich and generous constituency party, often have no help apart from the voluntary kind outside the House. Demands for increased constituency expenses are growing partly in response to the ever increasing 'social work' aspect of the MP's job, and partly because more and more members have come to the conclusion that, to be more efficient and effective, they need both a constituency office and one in Westminster.

ACCOMMODATION AND SUPPORT SERVICES

Whereas there may be all kinds of difficulties associated with MPs' rate of pay, there is less contention about the need to improve facilities. Most members are convinced that their efficiency is impaired by a desk in a corridor and a share of a 'phone. And there is no evidence that, where MPs are better accommodated, they necessarily become more grandiose and remote. It is not surprising that a considerable number of MPs look longingly at the empty GLC building across the water which could provide them with so much extra space, and support the idea of local authorities providing them with constituency offices and basic equipment.

Many members also think that they should be given better office equipment, including easy access to computers and fax machines, which would allow them to link up with their constituencies. As Michael Hirst put it,

> It is not just a matter of prestige, of wanting a better room, a bigger computer and so on to indicate status; rather the conditions actually hamper the functioning of an MP. . . . Better back-up would mean that the steam was taken out of the situation to some extent by the conditions being more conducive to efficiency, less conducive to heart attack.

Improvement in facilities (including the provision of a crèche) and in back-up services were often seen as more important than an increase in salary.

Some of those who suggested that secretarial and research allowances were more important than pay did so because they felt that MPs were not being efficiently used. They argued that, on arriving at Westminster, many MPs are vague about what goes on and tend to be defeated by the system unless they are exceptionally persistent. They are not given the assistance they need to do any part of the job properly. 'The problem', said one, 'is that politicians and their leaders are terrified of the public and feel that they shouldn't give themselves more money or more allowances. This may be stupid and self-defeating, but it is how members think.'

However, this argument has begun to be eroded as members see themselves unable to work efficiently without adequate accommodation and adequate secretarial and research allowances. And, a sign of the times, more and more of the 1980s' intakes, many of whom are not London-based and who, unlike their predecessors, know how homes are run, are demanding shopping facilities within or near the precincts of Westminster. As one of them put it, 'I have been in my flat for six months, but because of the ridiculous hours I work I still haven't found time to buy a plug for my television set.'

HOURS

The MP's job is not, and cannot be, a nine-to-five one. Like many other professional people, politicians carry their work round with them all the time, and there is no final hooter to indicate that the shift is over. More than most, too, they are public property, living much of their lives in the proverbial goldfish bowl. Attempts to control the job by limiting the hours are therefore conventionally dismissed by most MPs, and a certain scorn is reserved for those who suggest that, except in exceptional circumstances, morning sessions could obviate the need for late-night sittings, permitting, if not a nine-to-five, then something like a ten-to-eight routine. There is in the dismissal of reform here something of the martyr's acceptance of the crown of thorns; it may be extremely uncomfortable, but it certainly indicates commitment and worthiness for the job. The open-endedness of the hours of the House, however, sometimes leads to government by exhaustion, which is neither efficient nor necessary; and one does not have to be hypercritical to wonder if this is a case of those who are unsure of their role seeking purpose through activity. To members caught within the existing structures of debate, procedures can often seem immutable – 'Any reform would cause such a row that it wouldn't be worth the effort'; from outside, however, the defence of the all-night sitting seems much less convincing. As ex-MP David Marquand said, with the perspective of one who now looks in rather than out, 'people in lunatic asylums are probably very happy to be in a lunatic asylum. They want it to stay a lunatic asylum. It's the same way in the Palace of Westminster.'[6]

Every campaign to change parliamentary hours, and there have been several in recent years, has petered out unsuccessfully – not because MPs are all masochistically committed to the 'night shift', but because there is not sufficient unity of interest. Members whose homes and constituencies are outside London do not have the same incentive as those who live in or around the capital to stop work at 6 or 7 p.m. They use the House in the evening like a club, for its bars, smoking-room and restaurants, all set within the congenial context of professional political gossip. Again, there may also be, as one member put it, 'a bit of a generation gap'. Those new to the House are somewhat inhibited about criticising procedures; and, above all, they do not want to look as if they cannot stand the pace! Older members have learnt to live with the system and have often grown complacent in the process.

One reform, however, which has won general support is that a proper Timetabling Committee should be set up. This would allow MPs to know the House's programme well in advance, and not only, as at present, just a few days beforehand. Another popular reform would be the restricting of voting after 10 p.m. Late nights are seen by many members as a symptom of 'a silly boy scout's sense of duty in staying up all night'. It was nonsense, said one parliamentarian, to assume that the hours were unchangeable and that somehow lateness showed a commitment to the job. Many agreed that fixed parliamentary terms would also be a bonus, avoiding the present situation where members never know till the last moment when a recess is to begin and end.

On the other hand, most members were opposed to morning sittings, which could go some way towards solving the problem of late hours. It was argued that no one would attend them (perhaps because so many members are busy topping up their salaries elsewhere?) or that they would simply mean an even longer day for those who did participate. Others thought that morning sittings could easily be carried on concurrently with the committees of the House. A major problem about getting rid of late-night sittings, as many members pointed out, is that time may be the only weapon available to the opposition. If times were fixed, then the government of the day could never be caught napping and the opposition would be greatly weakened. As one member argued, 'There is an elasticity built into these long hours which allows Parliament to be always vigilant'. He believed this would be lost if the hours were more predictable. He had worked in a Cabinet minister's office and talked of the slight tension which was always there when the House was able to sit and ready to debate issues at short notice. This he thought was very healthy.

SELECT COMMITTEES

Even those MPs who agree that the straggling hours of the House should be pruned are divided about how it could be done. All the proposed changes – morning sittings, stricter timetabling, the enforcement of the ten o'clock vote and compulsory ten-minute speeches for everyone – have their detractors. It is certainly true that, under the current arrangements, and where the government has a large majority, the only weapon the opposition, and indeed the House as a whole, has against the strength of the government bulldozer is time. Any attempt to use time more efficiently would also mean, therefore, that the government would have even greater control than at present over the parliamentary timetable. So far, this fear, as much as the dead hand of tradition, has stopped reform in this area, and it seems that it will continue to do so in the future.

Almost all backbenchers approve of the development and strengthening of Select Committees. These have given members a new role and have encouraged the view that Parliament really does have some control over the administration. Suggestions that the Select Committees should be made more powerful, be given wider terms of reference and have their reports debated by the House as a matter of course are popular with MPs. And yet, important as they may be in developing backbench expertise in specific areas, they can often appear esoteric in their concerns and, rather than informing opinion in the House, become a coterie of experts talking to other experts.

In any case, they have not developed as some hoped they might, along the lines of the American Congressional Committees, which give their members a special kind of power and influence. The House of Commons is not the House of Representatives; MPs are not congressmen. The American system involves a fairly strict separation of powers where the administration does not need to, and often cannot, count on a majority in the House which asserts its own position informed by its committees. The Commons is there not only to review government policy, but, itself having provided the government from amongst its own members, also to support it. The jobs in the two institutions cannot be the same. MPs normally fulfil a number of roles which do not, perhaps, predispose them towards specialism, although some may come from a specialist background. Even if they like the idea of keeping a check on the executive, they are unlikely to allow this role to become the predominant backbench one. As one commentator has it, 'the political animal resents having to channel his energies in one particular direction for any length of time'.[10]

Nevertheless, a considerable number of members believe that Select Committees need to be strengthened. One suggestion already mentioned is that the House should debate their reports, and some have even argued that each such debate should end with a free vote. In the same vein, others have suggested what they called an 'extension of the system' – the more influence Select Committees have and the greater the part they play, even in the committee stages of Bills, the better. In this context, more authority to back their recommendations and greater specialist back-up for members are seen as integral to a reformed Select Committee system.

But other members were worried about the breadth and topicality of the subjects which Select Committees discuss. Their solution was to limit the topics under review. Selectivity, they argued, would strengthen the committees' workings. The right to call civil servants and ministers to give evidence before them also needed to be reinforced. Some members went further in suggesting that the whips should not be able to influence the composition of Select Committees. The very general nature of the committees, their often vague terms of reference and their apparent lack of direction were deprecated by one MP, who wanted clear objectives and priorities to be established by Parliament at the start of any investigation; a discussion and evaluation of progress before the draft-report stage was reached; and a greater effort by chairmen to accommodate opposing views (in minority statements and so on). Yet others wondered if it would be possible to give Select Committees a pre-legislative role – that is, the right to discuss the basic principles of proposed Bills. Overall, proposals for change pointed in the direction of strengthening the current Select Committee procedures and giving more weight to the reports and recommendations of committees.

Three main recommendations for strengthening the role of the Select Committees emerge. Firstly, they ought to have full powers 'to send for persons, papers and records'. In the 1980s the Westland affair again showed that governments can still refuse Select Committees access to its minutes and civil servants. Secondly, special days should be set aside for debating Committee reports on the floor of the House. Thirdly, as the 1977–78 Procedure Committee suggested, Select Committee Chairmen should be paid 'a modest additional salary' and Select Committee members be entitled to an extra research allowance. Finally, there seems little doubt that once the television cameras are in place the authority of, and interest in, the Select Committees will be enhanced.

QUESTION TIME

Members were asked specifically how Question Time, and Prime Minister's Question Time in particular, could be improved – for example, by extending the time set aside for it; or by making it an open session, without notice of questions having to be given; or by submission of questions the day before, with supplementaries permitted.

A majority of backbenchers (60.4 per cent) were dissatisfied with Prime Minister's Question Time. A breakdown by party shows, not surprisingly, 47.7 per cent of Conservatives, but only 28.9 per cent of Labour members, satisfied. As for the Alliance, the group most likely to be adversely affected by the gladiatorial two-party structure of the present Question Time, none of its members was satisfied.

The incidence of dissatisfaction rose steeply with age; only a quarter of those aged 30 or less were dissatisfied, but the proportion rose to 52.7 per cent for members aged 31–40, 57.7 per cent for those in the 41–50 age bracket, and 78.1 per cent for the over fifties. The youngest members (mainly Tories) appeared to enjoy a good shout.

The complaints about Prime Minister's Question Time ranged from 'doesn't elicit real information' to an accusation that it was 'ritualistic'. As one commentator put it, 'it's a triumph of enquiry over information'. Others were equally disparaging in other ways: 'creates more heat than light'; 'more "playtime" than Question Time'; 'tedious, noisy, unstructured, trite and largely inaudible'; 'truth the first casualty of enquiry'. Those who were satisfied, however, stated that it was a 'reasonable opportunity to raise issues of political importance'; that 'its existence constitutes a valuable democratic opportunity to examine Britain's chief executive and provides an immediate opportunity to air current matters of concern'. Further, it was 'an important opportunity to gauge backbench opinion and judge performance'.

Members were also asked to provide their suggestions for improving Question Time. One idea was that the Prime Minister should have notice of questions but that departmental issues could also be raised, with the relevant minister assisting the Prime Minister. Another idea was 'a rota for Questions plus the Speaker's choice for further Questions'. A 'Cabinet Question Time' (perhaps one hour on Thursdays) was suggested, and found favour with some. Another suggestion was that the Leader of the Opposition should only be allowed one question, thus taking much of the heat out of the whole affair. A deeply pessimistic attitude, not altogether uncommon among members, was reflected in one member's comment: 'Question Time has sunk so low that it is probably now beyond rescue.'

Making Prime Minister's Question Time into a Select Committee of the whole House under the Speaker's chairmanship, thus enabling important topics to be explored in depth, was another radical suggestion. Again, the idea that all Privy Councillors should be barred from asking questions 'until at least four backbenchers had been called' reflects backbench dissatisfaction with the current arrangements for questioning the government. (Privy Councillors are, of course, given priority both in debates and at Question Time.)

ATTENDANCE IN THE CHAMBER: DEBATES

In the All-Party Reform Group questionnaire, MPs were asked to suggest ways in which attendance in the Chamber could be increased; whether they thought low attendance a problem (the majority did) and, if so, why they thought attendance was so poor and how they thought this could be remedied.

Breakdown by party showed wide differences in rates of satisfaction. 73.2 per cent of centre parties' members were satisfied. The proportion dropped to 59.6 per cent for Conservatives and 47 per cent for Labour members. Again, satisfaction decreased with age: 83 per cent of members aged 40 or less were not worried by the poor attendance, but only 51.3 per cent of respondents aged 41–61 were similarly unconcerned. Younger parliamentarians, it seems, because they had known nothing else, accepted low attendance in the Chamber as normal. Those with longer memories remembered what they believed to be better times. The figures probably also reflect an opposition which feels itself stifled and undermined by a permanent and seemingly invincible government majority.

There was general agreement that poor attendances were the result of the demands made by office and committee work, coupled with members' frustration at the slim chance of being called to speak. (One MP estimated that a backbencher was likely, on average, to make only four speeches a year.) Offices, too, were often far from the Chamber, again inhibiting easy attendance. Shorter speeches (particularly by Privy Councillors) were high on the list of suggested improvements here; morning sittings were again put forward as a possible way of increasing speaking-time, so encouraging more members into the Chamber.

In every context, the length of speeches was widely criticised. A new Conservative member admitted that 'one recognises the Opposition's right to oppose, but somehow we must evolve a system that controls mindless time-wasting by limiting speeches in report stage and when a Bill is in a Committee of the Whole House and, indeed, for contributions in Standing Committee'. Very much on the same lines, a Conservative MP of twenty-five years' standing suggested,

> push some of the minor legislation out of the Chamber into a committee room upstairs – the number involved in debate on the floor of the House is often so small it is about the same size as a Committee anyway! Why should twenty people be allowed to keep hundreds of others up all night, night after night? This is an abuse!

But another long-serving member, perhaps with a hankering for an idealised golden past, declared, 'We need a less partisan atmosphere: less point-scoring and more reasoned argument. The opposition of the day (of whatever party) should rely less on trying to delay government business and more on arguing its case. We should have fewer votes. . . .'

A stricter use of the whip's office to encourage members to listen to debates was put forward by one parliamentarian, while another suggested a more radical solution: 'allow MPs to opt for a part-time status on their present salary or full-time status on a far greater salary'. It is difficult to see how this would help, unless the new full-time 'contract' stipulated a minimum number of hours to be spent in the Chamber. Other draconian measures included the suggestion that the existing Standing Order forbidding the reading of speeches should be enforced (presumably on the assumption that, if they had to memorise their ideas before they started, most MPs would be commendably brief). Speeches containing no reference to previous speeches in the proceedings should, it has been suggested, also be ruled out of order, as simply isolated statements rather than a contribution to a general debate. In July 1988 members of the House of Commons voted (typically, in the small hours) to limit backbench (but not Privy Councillors') speeches in major debates to 10 minutes, a reform which, it has been calculated, will allow three or four more backbenchers to speak in the big debates.

SPOKESMAN FOR LOCAL INTERESTS

We come finally to the role of the MP as his or her constituents' representative. This aspect of an MP's job is believed, as we have seen, to have encroached more and more on members' time. This is a result partly of the growing complexities of the modern bureaucratic system with which constituents have to deal, and partly of the very public role most MPs play in their constituencies. Members hold frequent surgeries, write for the local newspapers, and generally attempt to achieve a higher local profile than before. The volatility of the electorate puts all but the very safest seats at risk. Reselection in the Labour Party means that Labour politicians consciously set out to be seen and heard more frequently in their constituencies; Conservatives, many in the newly created marginals of 1983, hope to keep their seats and must work at them accordingly; and the centre parties, always afraid of being squeezed out by the two major parties, have to remain vigilant and vigorous.

But do members believe that there has been a significant increase in constituency workload? And, if so, how have they reacted to this? We asked a number of MPs from the 1974 intake how, if at all, things had changed for them since then. These members had taken part in the Hansard Society's 1974 survey of newly elected members, and their answers then were compared with their views now.

They were asked if they felt that voters had increasingly come to expect their MP to take up personal cases, and, if so, whether this was a trend they approved. The majority of those interviewed agreed that this was the trend and were uneasy about it, though for rather different reasons. One member saw the problem not so much in terms of the strain placed on MPs as in terms of the increasing inability of constituents to obtain satisfaction from the relevant local authority. Similarly, another believed that most of his cases could have been dealt with by local people at the local level. A third thought that MPs should be a 'last resort', but, because local councillors had a low profile between elections, the MP often carried the responsibility for this type of work. As most members agreed, what disturbed them was not so much the extra workload as the unbalancing of the job in the direction of the local rather than the national constituency. Taking the argument even further, some of those interviewed suggested that it had become all too easy to opt out of real responsibility at Westminster by immersion in constituency work.

However, several members felt strongly that constituents rightly expected their MP to look after their needs. Society had become very complex, they argued, and democracy was more fragile than people realised. In this context it was crucial to connect ordinary people with the system, otherwise government became remote and faceless. Indeed, at least one MP who in 1974 had thought that constituency demands were too great had changed his mind and now believed that the member ought to be aware of and involved with constituents' personal problems, even if these were finally dealt with by others. Still, all agreed that a balance had to be struck between being a good constituency member and being the national representative at Westminster. Only the MP could play the national political role, whereas others (councillors, social workers, and so on) could perform the social-welfare function. On the other hand, people now expected all MPs to be interested in the latter, and, as we have seen, members themselves were often content to emphasise this aspect of the job.

Most of those who welcomed the constituency based job did so not only because, idealistically, they thought such concerns right and proper, but also because they believed, pragmatically, that it gave their role a firmer base – it 'keeps your feet on the ground'. Politicians, they said, needed to know the reality of people's lives, and without such involvements they might become isolated and inward-looking. They might also be light on constituency support at the election, which was never more than five years away.

THE ELECTORAL SYSTEM

There is one reform which might change the balance of the MP's job, by changing the make-up of the Commons – the reform of the electoral system. We have already noted that a system of pro-portional representation could, for example, encourage the selec-tion of more women and black candidates, which might in itself alter the predominant concerns of the very largely white, male House. This is not necessarily to suggest that there are clear-cut 'female politics' or 'black politics', but simply to note that the experiences and lifestyles of these groups are rather different from those of the present membership, and these might be reflected not only in policies but in style. There is now some evidence to suggest, for example, that women operate in a public context rather differently from men, that their perception of the nature of 'politics' is different from the male view,[11] and that there is an identifiable 'gender gap' between the political priorities of the sexes.[12] More women in the Commons would no doubt point up these differences, and this might modify the backbench job itself.

The possibility of such change, however, is slim so long as either of the two largest parties has a working majority in the House. Probably only the intervention of the centre parties, which are committed to proportional representation, returned in much increased strength and holding the balance of power, could force one of the other two main parties, in return for support in the House, to adopt a proportional system. At the moment, there is little desire among members to abandon the single-member, first-past-the-post system, and a recent survey carried out by the University of Reading showed more than four-fifths of MP respon-dents satisfied with the present arrangements.[13]

TELEVISING PARLIAMENT

The televising of Parliament will, it is argued by some, inevitably change the whole balance of the backbench job. On the face of it, however, this may seem unlikely. Sound broadcasting of the Chamber has not, after all, revolutionised the MP's role. Indeed, as Professor Blumler, Director of Leeds University Centre for Televi-sion Research, says, 'the sound broadcasting of Parliament has been neither a resounding success nor a disaster, but something of an anti-climax when faced against the expectations that were aired before and during its introduction'.[14] Others, however, argue that televising Parliament will entice MPs out of their offices and the committee rooms back into the Chamber, so as to be seen to be engaging in debate on the great issues of the day. After all, says Bryan Gould MP, members know that television is the most important medium of communication today and indicate this 'by abandoning the Chamber for the chance of a brief appearance on television ... because they know that ... it is essential to communicate with the electorate and television is the way to do it.'[15]

It used to be argued that it was perhaps unrealistic and romantic to believe that the Chamber could become again, if indeed it ever was, the centre of parliamentary life. Too much of the MP's job now has its focus outside the Chamber and often away from the House; Select Committees have assumed much of the work of checking the executive; legislative detail is largely decided in Standing Committees; and the constituency, for most MPs, forever calls. It may be significant that when members debated the televising of the House of Commons in November 1985, the argument was not in terms of reviving the flagging fortunes of the Chamber, but in terms of the impact of the arc lamps on the backbench psyche. John Stokes, Conservative member for Halesowen and Stourbridge, argued that television was 'essentially a branch of show business' and would inevitably trivialise political debate.[16] For once there was some cross-party agreement, and Joe Ashton, Labour member for Bassetlaw, claimed that the cameras would simply turn the Commons into what he picturesquely described as 'Scrap of the Day'. In the end, although there was widespread support for televising, mostly on the basis that the House ought to be prepared to drag itself into the twentieth century, the decision went against it by 12 votes.

But times change. Three years later, in February 1988, the issue was raised again, and, despite the personal opposition of the Prime Minister, the old guard were defeated by the large majority of 54 in a free vote. Despite the usual warning that television cameras would manipulate the House, encourage bad behaviour, and trivialise debates, the new intake of 1987, young and unimpressed by the caution of their seniors, accepted the arguments of those who said that it would give the House of Commons the opportunity once again to become the central forum for political debate in Britain. Michael Heseltine, former Defence Secretary, summed up the majority view perhaps, when he stated in the debate: 'Parliament has taken the opportunity to ensure that when the great political issues come up they will be exposed on the floor of the Chamber without interpretation and without media gloss for the judgement of the public. They will see the warts but that will be far more than compensated for by the excellence of parliamentary occasion.'

In addition, the televising of the Chamber and some Select Committees, may well produce another, and perhaps just as desirable, side-effect. It will tend to encourage a healthy independence on the part of backbenchers who will now be able to appeal over the heads of the whips. The backbencher as lobby fodder and little else, may well become a thing of the past.

FURTHER REFORMS

When the All-Party Reform Group asked for general comments on changes which members would like to see implemented, it elicited some fairly radical suggestions. A Liberal complained that 'the UK Parliament has completely lost its way. It remains exactly like a nineteenth-century debating-chamber, in a modern society which is now immensely complex. We should deliberately adopt many modern features from other parliaments in the world, especially from Europe.' In somewhat similar vein, a Labour MP declared, 'turn the Palace of Westminster into a museum and build a modern legislature with twentieth-century facilities elsewhere. If pressed for a location, how about Oldham?'

Many MPs argued for better facilities and conditions:

> There are virtually no social facilities at Westminster when one considers the length of time members spend in the place. Possibly something could be arranged if non-essential people, such as research assistants, were restricted to outbuildings. It might even be desirable to restrict the press.

And, a cry from the heart on a muggy summer's day: 'air conditioning!'

Another member, however, was unimpressed by such simplistic solutions, suggesting that, although it was right to look for improvements in the system,

> my experience over the years suggests [to me] that the end result

depends more upon how members use the system than the system itself. The really serious problem is that too many MPs have a marked lack of interest in any but their own speeches. That has grown up in inverse proportion to the ever-increasing provision of services and facilities for Members.

This pessimism was echoed by others: 'I suppose things would only change when people in the Commons change. But since MPs are by definition peculiar individuals – so Parliament will retain its peculiar characteristics.' Some apparently glory in this 'peculiarity', and at least one member went on to encourage the All-Party Reform Group not to upset the *status quo*: 'don't meddle too much, avoid further inroads by the media. Be loyal to Parliament – which means backing the Speaker.' Not much scope for change there.

Of those convinced of the need for change, however, many suggested a combination of wide procedural reform and detailed administrative adjustments. One Conservative reduced it all conveniently to four simple issues:

One, announce the business of the House two weeks ahead; two, centralise arrangements for visits to the House, so MPs and staff do not have to waste time organising these; three, computerise ticket allocation to the Strangers' Gallery so that swaps are facilitated; four, introduce self-sealing, prepared envelopes!

An older member had the requirement down to three: 'Abolish research assistants. Don't sit after 10 p.m. Get a decent chef in the kitchen'.

But many take these problems very seriously. A young Liberal was deeply critical:

Parliament as presently constituted is a sick joke. If something is not done to improve the way it is run, I will either spend far more time in my constituency, where I feel I have a very positive part to play in local affairs, or pack the whole thing in and earn an honest living elsewhere.

Despite interest in and commitment to their jobs, members of Parliament have no trouble in suggesting reforms which they feel need to be implemented. And, if on the one hand one can appreciate the breadth of the reforms suggested, on the other one cannot help but feel that the main reason why so few of them have been considered is exactly their disparate nature. In the end, a lack of consensus among MPs themselves on what needs to be done and, more importantly, a failure to set priorities as between such measures, has meant that those who oppose reform as too radical or too inconvenient have been able to divide and rule, thus maintaining the *status quo*.

We have seen how the job of an MP has been modified in the recent past, both by external pressures and by internal political changes. Increasing 'professionalisation', brought about largely by the need to meet the demands of constituencies and the extension of politics into almost every area of modern life, has meant that the appeal of the job is perhaps narrower than ever before. Politicians, to succeed and survive, have to be more determined, single-minded, better organised and more ruthless than in the past. As can be seen from MPs' diaries, the life of politics does not allow for much compromise with a life outside. As a *Guardian* editorial has put it,

> Politics, the whole politics and nothing but politics: that is the essential road to salvation. And if you stubbornly persist in leading an orthodox life, if you refuse to sacrifice all other interests ... then you are held under this dispensation to have forfeited your right to influence the fate of your party.[17]

Such obsessive dedication appeals only to the few, and, although, on one level, it may indicate laudable commitment, it is not costless. It severely limits the number of those prepared to play the game and consequently isolates them from those they represent. Many MPs are themselves aware of this: 'the longer members are in the House, the more they are divorced from reality', says Anthony Nelson MP, himself a veteran with some twelve years' service.

Total dedication is required, it seems, less for the results it achieves than for the indication it gives that the participant is playing by the rules and deserves to succeed. According to Shirley Summerskill, the reason why there are so few women in politics is that generally they are unwilling or unable to give this complete dedication, and allow other parts of their lives to intrude into politics: 'I have seen a busy woman minister preoccupied with buying tomatoes ("because we have run out at home").'[18] The implication here is that politics is, and ought to be, hermetically sealed from everyday life; it is, and ought to be, an activity in which participants think great thoughts and make important decisions – and where nobody buys tomatoes. On the other hand, it might be argued that we could do with more politicians who live in the real, tomato-buying world.

We shall not get them, of course, within the present structures, where MPs are increasingly, as we have seen, career politicians, in the House for a large part of their working lives. But if that is so, then those working lives need to be run more efficiently and with fewer outmoded and counter-productive rules and regulations. As one member has stated, 'The way in which we work is unplanned and uncoordinated and suits only the government, not Parliament.'

A good example is the account, in the summer of 1988, of a newly-elected Tory MP who described his antics trying to introduce a Ten Minute Rule Bill. 'I have to sit in the room opposite the Public Bill Office for 24 hours except for an hour or so for lunch, tea and dinner, if I am relieved by a colleague. There are no facilities of any sort. I can't make a cup of coffee and even if I want to go to the loo I have to leave a note. I have to sleep there too and as the room is air-conditioned it is freezing. This procedure as it stands is arcane, archaic and ridiculous.'

Reforms need to be taken seriously. The long, and often unnecessary, late hours make the House of Commons 'the most sophisticated political prison in the world'. Parliament meets for more days than any other legislature in the world and has the longest and latest hours. Backbenchers now accept that reforms here are long overdue. As we have seen, the business of the House, the 1980s' intakes have argued, could be properly timetabled and should finish at 10 p.m. Adjournment debates, now that television has arrived, could begin at 1 p.m. so that important local issues could be properly aired; recesses could be shorter and the dates of sittings at least provisionally agreed for the whole year at the start of the session.

Reforms of staffing and facilities, of parliamentary procedures, of public expenditure accounts, and of Select Committees would not only strengthen the hand of the backbencher by allowing him to play a greater part in the legislative process, but would also ensure that Parliament performs the role which it is expected to carry out. Select Committees should have their major reports debated, have the power to order the attendance of Ministers and civil servants before them, and, it has been suggested, be able to insist on a review or cooling-off period during which Government Bills could be scrutinised before going to a Committee of the whole House. A report to the Treasury Select Committee in July 1988 also proposed that, given the hiving off of some civil service departments into separate agencies, the top management of the latter should be expected, as part of the process of democratic accountability, to appear before the Select Committee.

However, even if most backbenchers support reforms, or even accept that without them they are simply at the mercy of the government of the day, their fascination with politics is such that, once caught they can never free themselves from the pull of Westminster. The pleasure of politics felt by the addicted, despite the frustrations, never falters. It is in the intoxicating feeling of being at the centre of things, of making things happen, of contributing to decisions that matter and, should this all seem too egocentric, of helping people. These, in some combination, are what the job has always been about and, in spite of the changes in how it might be done, probably always will be. Most of the changes members discussed would merely hone the tools they already possess to do their current jobs of scrutineers at Westminster and welfare officers in the constituencies. The changes are essentially of the 'tinkering' variety and could be accommodated within present structures and procedures. Whether the necessary consensus even for those could be won, however, is dubious. As the *Economist* put it: 'MPs ... have not yet learned to act collectively in their own interest against the interests of the front benches of both major parties. If ever a man has suffered through not belonging to a trade union it has been the modern MP.'[19] The 1986 revolt on allowances may signal something of a change in this, however, and it certainly illustrates what members working together on their own behalf can achieve.

The wider question is increasingly posed, more outside the House than in it however, as to whether we need clarification of the role of Parliament itself. Such change is demanded, for example, by the advocates of a written constitution. It may be that as we approach the year 2000, and more immediately, as Parliament faces the new challenge of the European Single Market and closer European integration, that the time has come for a Royal Commission to give a redefinition of the House's proper role in government. Out of such an analysis could come a more comprehensive and comprehensible idea of the role we expect our MPs to play, perhaps at the same time encouraging a greater public awareness of both the limitations and the possibilities of the backbench job.

NOTES

1. *HC Deb.*, 119, col. 168, 6 July 1987.
2. *TSRB report*, Cmnd. II, p. 26.
3. *HC Deb.*, 119, col. 168, 6 July 1897.
4. Peter Hennessy, The *Independent*, 13 June 1988.
5. A. Mitchell, 'Consulting the Workers: MPs on their Jobs', *Parliamentarian*, Jan 1985.
6. P. Wilding, *Professional Power and Social Welfare* (Routledge & Kegan Paul, 1982) p. 95.
7. 640 members were elected in 1945, 625 in 1950, 630 in 1955 and 635 in 1974. See D. Butler and A. Sloman, *British Electoral Facts 1900–1979* (Macmillan, 1980).
8. All figures are for the last election in each country. The French figure includes representatives of overseas departments as well as of metropolitan France.
9. Quoted in A. Mitchell, *Westminster Man: A Tribal Anthropology of the Commons People* (Methuen, 1982) p. 272.
10. T. A. Smith, *Anti Politics: Consensus Reform and Protest in Britain* (Charles Knight, 1972) p. 150.
11. *Women and Men of Europe in 1983*, supplement no. 16 to *Women of Europe* (Commission of the European Communities, 1983) pp. 43–5.
12. See P. Norris, 'The Gender Gap in Britain and America', *Parliamentary Affairs*, 38, no. 3 (1985).
13. K. Gladdish, A. Liddell and P. Giddings, *MPs' Perceptions of the British Electoral System* (University of Reading, 1985).
14. J. Blumler, 'The Sound of Parliament', *Parliamentary Affairs*, 37, no. 3 (1984) 263.
15. B. Gould, 'Televise Parliament to Revive the Chamber', *Parliamentary Affairs*, 37, no. 3 (1984) 248.
16. For accounts of the debate, see, for example, *The Times* and *Guardian*, 21 Nov 1985, and *The Sunday Times*, 24 Nov 1985.
17. *Guardian*, 29 Oct 1982.
18. S. Summerskill, 'Nineteen in the House', *Listener*, 17 Jan 1980.
19. *Economist*, March 1988.

Bibliography

BOOKS AND PAMPHLETS

Abse, L., *Private Member* (Macdonald, 1973).

Alderman, G., *British Elections: Myth and Reality* (Batsford, 1979).

Bagehot, W., *The English Constitution*, 12th edn (Oxford University Press, 1963).

Ball, A., *British Political Parties* (Macmillan, 1981).

Barber, J., *The Lawmakers: Recruitment and Adoption in Legislative Life* (Yale University Press, 1965).

Barker, A., and Rush, M., *The Member of Parliament and his Information* (Allen and Unwin, 1970).

Barnett, J., *Inside the Treasury* (André Deutsch, 1982).

Beloff, M., and Peele, G., *The Government of the United Kingdom: Political Authority in a Changing Society* (Weidenfeld and Nicolson, 1980).

Berrington, H., *Backbench Opinion in the House of Commons* (Pergamon Press, 1973).

Birch, A. H., *The British System of Government*, 2nd edn (Allen and Unwin, 1968).

Blondel, J., *Comparative Legislatures* (Prentice Hall, 1973).

Bogdanor, V., *What is Proportional Representation?* (Martin Robertson, 1984).

—— (ed.), *Representatives of the People? Parliamentarians and Constituencies in Modern Democracies* (Gower Press, 1985).

Borthwick, R., and Spence, J. (eds), *British Parties in Perspective* (Leicester University Press, 1984).

Buck, P., *Amateurs and Professionals in British Politics, 1918–59* (University of Chicago Press, 1963).

Butler, D., and Kavanagh, D. (eds), *The British General Election of February 1974* (Macmillan, 1974).

——, *The British General Election of 1979* (Macmillan, 1980).

Butler, D., and Sloman, A., *British Political Facts 1900–1979* (Macmillan 1980).

Butler, D., and Stokes, D., *Political Change in Britain* (Macmillan, 1969).

Butt, R., *The Power of Parliament* (Constable, 1969).

Colquhoun, M., *Woman in the House* (Scan Books, 1980).

Craig, F. W. S., *British Electoral Facts* (Macmillan, 1976).

Crewe, I., *British MPs and their Constituencies: How Strong are the Links?* Essex Papers in Politics and Government no. 10 (University of Essex, 1984).

Crick, B., *The Reform of Parliament* (Weidenfeld and Nicolson, 1964).

Critchley, J., *Westminster Blues: Minor Chords* (Elm Tree Books/Hamish Hamilton, 1985).

Crossman, R., *Backbench Diaries of Richard Crossman*, ed. J. Morgan (Hamish Hamilton/Cape, 1981).

——, *Diaries of a Cabinet Minister*, 3 vols (Hamish Hamilton, 1975–7).

——, *Introduction to Bagehot's English Constitution*, 4th edn (Fontana, 1965).

Cunningham, G., *Careers in Politics* (Kogan Page, 1984).

Dahrendorf, R., *The New Liberty – Survival and Justice in a Changing World* (Routledge and Kegan Paul, 1975).

Dicey, A. V., *The Law of the Constitution* (Macmillan, 1908).

Dod's Parliamentary Companion, 1986 edn.

Doig, A., *Corruption and Misconduct in Contemporary British Politics* (Penguin, 1984).

Drewry, G. (ed.), *The New Select Committees: A Study of the 1979 Reforms* (Oxford University Press, 1985).

Drucker, H. (ed.), *Developments in British Politics* (Macmillan, 1983).

Englefield, D. (ed.), *Commons Select Committees: Catalysts for Progress?* (Longman, 1984).

Erskine May, Sir Thomas, *The Constitutional History of England* (Longmans Green, 1912).

——, *Parliamentary Practice*, 20th edn (Butterworth, 1983).

Fairlie, H., *The Life of Politics* (Methuen, 1968).

Fell, B., and Mackenzie, K. R., *The Houses of Parliament* (Eyre and Spottiswoode, 1977).

Gladdish, K., Liddell, O., and Giddings, P., *MPs' Perceptions of the British Electoral System* (University of Reading, 1985).

Goehlert, R. U., and Martin, F. S., *The Parliament of Great Britain: A Bibliography* (Lexington Books, 1983).

Gordon, S., *Our Parliament* (Cassell, 1964).

Grant, J., *The Member of Parliament* (Michael Joseph, 1974).

Greenleaf, W. H., *The British Political Tradition*, 2 vols (Methuen, 1983).

Gregory, R., and Hutchesson, P., *The Parliamentary Ombudsman: A Study in the Control of Administrative Action* (Allen and Unwin, for Royal Institute of Public Administration, 1975).

Guttsman, W. L., *The British Political Elite* (McGibbon and Kee, 1963).

Halsley, A. (ed.), *Trends in British Society since 1900* (Macmillan, 1972).

Hanson, A. H., and Crick, B. (eds), *The Commons in Transition* (Collins, 1970).

Hanson, A. H., and Wells, M., *Governing Britain* (Fontana, 1981).

Herbert, A. P., *Independent Member* (Methuen, 1950).

Holland, P., *Lobby Fodder – the Role of the Backbencher in Parliament* (Harvester Press, 1988).

Holme, R. and Elliot, M. (eds), *Time for a New Constitution, 1688–1988* (Macmillan, 1988).

Ilbert, C., *Parliament, its History, Constitution, and Practice* (Home University Library, 1929).

Jackson, J. A. (ed.), *Professions and Professionalization* (Cambridge University Press, 1970).

James, R. R., *The House of Commons* (Collins, 1961).

Jenkins, W. I., *Policy Analysis* (Martin Robertson, 1978).

Jennings, I., *Parliament* (Cambridge University Press, 1969).

Jowett, R., and Airey, C., *British Social Attitudes: The 1984 Report* (Gower Press, 1984).

Judge, D., *Backbench Specialisation in the House of Commons* (Heinemann, 1981).

—— (ed.), *The Politics of Parliamentary Reform* (Gower, 1983).

Kilmuir, Lord, *Political Adventure* (Weidenfeld and Nicolson, 1964).

King, A., *British Members of Parliament: A Self-Portrait* (Macmillan for Granada TV, 1974).

——, *Sex, Money and Power: Political Scandals in Great Britain and the US*, Essex Papers in Politics and Government, no. 14 (University of Essex, 1984).

Lakeman, E., *Power to Elect* (Heinemann, 1982).

Lapping, B. (ed.), *The State of the Nation: Parliament* (Granada TV Publications, 1973)

Leonard, R., and Herman, V., *The Backbencher and Parliament* (Macmillan, 1973).

Lewis, R., and Maude, A., *Professional People* (Phoenix House, 1952).

Leys, C., *Politics in Britain: An Introduction* (Heinemann, 1983).

Mackintosh, J. P., *Government and Politics of Britain*, 5th edn (Hutchinson, 1982).

——, *On Parliament and Social Democracy* (Longman, 1982).

—— (ed.), *People and Parliament* (Saxon House, 1978).

Marsh, D., and Read, M., *British Private Members Balloted Bills*, Essex Papers in Politics and Government, no. 21 (University of Essex, 1985).

Marshall, E., *Parliament and the Public* (Macmillan, 1982).

Mayhew, C., *Party Games* (Hutchinson, 1969).

Mellors, C., *The British Member of Parliament: A Socio-Economic Survey* (Saxon House, 1978).

Menhennet, D., and Palmer, J., *Parliament in Perspective* (Bodley Head, 1967).

Mitchell, A., *Westminster Man: A Tribal Anthropology of the Commons People* (Methuen, 1982).

Moran, Lord, *Winston Churchill. The Struggle for Survival, 1940–65* (Constable, 1966).

Morris, A., *The Growth of Parliamentary Scrutiny by Committee* (Pergamon Press, 1970).

Morrison of Lambeth, Lord, *Government and Parliament*, 3rd edn (Oxford University Press, 1965).

Muller, W., *The Kept Men* (Harvester Press, 1977).

Nicolson, N., *People and Parliament* (Weidenfeld and Nicolson, 1958).

Norton, P., *The Commons in Perspective* (Martin Robertson, 1981).

Penniman, H. (ed.), *The General Election of 1979* (American Enterprise Institute for Public Policy, 1981).

Punnett, M., *British Government and Politics*, 4th edn (Heinemann, 1980).

Radice, L., *Reform of the House of Commons*, Fabian Tract 448 (1977).

Ramsey, M., 'An Introduction into how Britain is Governed', *Report of the Commission on the Constitution*, Cmnd 5460 (HMSO, 1973).

Richards, P. G., *Honourable Members* (Faber and Faber, 1959).

——, *The Backbenchers* (Faber and Faber, 1972).

Richardson, J. J., and Jordan, A. G., *Governing under Pressure* (Martin Robertson, 1979).

Rose, P., *The Backbencher's Dilemma* (Frederick Muller, 1981).

Rose, R., *Politics in England* (Faber and Faber, 1980).

Roth, A., *The Business Background of MPs* (Parliamentary Profiles, 1981).

Rush, M., *Selection of Parliamentary Candidates* (Nelson, 1969).

—— (ed.), *The House of Commons, Services and Facilities, 1972–1982* (PSI, 1983).
Rush, M., and Shaw, M., *The House of Commons: Services and Facilities* (Allen and Unwin, 1974).
Ryle, M. and Richards, P., (eds), *The Commons under Scrutiny* (Routledge, 1988).
Smith, T. A., *Anti Politics: Consensus, Reform and Protest in Britain* (Charles Knight, 1972).
St John Stevas, N., *Walter Bagehot* (Eyre and Spottiswoode, 1985).
Stanworth, P., and Giddens, A. (eds), *Elites and Power in British Society* (Cambridge University Press, 1974).
Stevens, O., *Children Talking Politics* (Martin Robertson, 1982).
Taylor, E., *The House of Commons at Work* (Penguin, 1951).
Taverne, D., *The Future of the Left* (Cape, 1974).
The Times Guide to the House of Commons (Times Books Ltd, 1983).
Vallance, E., *Women in the House: A Study of Women Members of Parliament* (Athlone Press, 1979).
Wade, E. C. S., and Phillips, G. G., *Constitutional Law*, 5th edn (Longmans Green, 1957).
Walkland, S. A. (ed.), *The House of Commons in the Twentieth Century* (Oxford University Press, 1979).
Walkland, S. A., and Ryle, M., *The Commons Today* (Fontana, 1981).
Westergaard, J., and Prester, H., *Class in a Capitalist Society* (Basic Books, 1952).
Wilding, N., and Laundy, P., *An Encyclopaedia of Parliament*, 3rd edn (Cassell, 1968).
Wilding, P., *Professional Power and Social Welfare* (Routledge and Kegan Paul, 1982).
Willey, F., *The Honourable Member* (Sheldon, 1974).
Wilson, H., *The Governance of Britain* (Weidenfeld and Nicolson, 1976).
Winterton, Lord, *Orders of the Day* (Cassell, 1953).
Women and Men of Europe in 1983, supplement no. 16 to *Women of Europe* (Commission of the European Communities, 1983).
Wyatt, W., *Turn Again, Westminster* (André Deutsch, 1973).

ARTICLES AND PAPERS

Barber, B., 'Some Problems in the Sociology of Professions', *Daedalus*, 92, no. 4 (1963).
Blumler, J., 'The Sound of Parliament', *Parliamentary Affairs*, 37, no. 3 (1984).
Bochel, J., and Denver, M., 'Candidates' Selection in the Labour Party; What the Selectors Seek', *British Journal of Political Science*, 13, no. 1 (1983).
Burch, M., and Moran, M., 'The Changing British Political Elite 1945–83: MPs and Cabinet Ministers', *Parliamentary Affairs*, 38, no. 1 (1985).
Couzens, K. E., 'A Minister's Correspondence', *Public Administration*, 34 (1956).
Crewe, I., and Spence, J., 'Parliament and Public', *New Society*, July 1973.
Eadie, H., 'The Helping Personality', *Contact* 49 (Summer 1975).

Evans, R., 'MPs Forced into More Post-Midnight Sittings', *The Times*, 25 Feb 1985.

Finch, S. E., 'The Mystery of Labour's Lost Votes', *The Times Higher Education Supplement*, 13 Dec. 1985.

Gould, B., 'Televise Parliament to Revive the Chamber', *Parliamentary Affairs*, 37, no. 3 (1984).

Hills, J., 'Candidates: The Impact of Gender', *Parliamentary Affairs*, 34, no. 2 (1981).

Holland, M., 'The Selection of Parliamentary Candidates', *Parliamentary Affairs*, 34, no. 1 (1981).

Ingle, S., 'Socialism and Literature: The Contribution of Imaginative Writers to the Development of the British Labour Party', *Political Studies*, 1974.

Ionescu, G., 'The Shrinking World of Bagehot', *Government and Opposition*, 10, no. 1 (1975).

Jones, G. W., 'The House of Commons: A Threat to Good Government?', *London Review of Public Administration*, 16 (1984).

Judge, D., 'The Politics of MPs' Pay', *Parliamentary Affairs*, 37, no. 1 (1984).

——, 'Specialists and Generalists in British Central Government: A Political Debate', *Public Administration*, 59 (1981).

King, A., 'The Rise of the Career Politician in Britain – and its Consequences', *British Journal of Political Science*, II, pt III (July 1981).

Knight, R., 'Changes in the Occupational Structure of the Working Population', *Journal of the Royal Statistical Society*, 1967.

Mitchell, A., 'Consulting the Workers: MPs on their Jobs', *Parliamentarian*, Jan 1985.

Norris, P., 'The Gender Gap in Britain and America', *Parliamentary Affairs*, 38, no. 3 (1985).

Norton, P., 'Dear Minister ... The Importance of MP to Minister Correspondence', *Parliamentary Affairs*, 35, no. 1 (1982).

——, 'Party Organisation in the House of Commons', *Parliamentary Affairs*, 31, no. 4 (1978).

Pimlott, B., 'How to Middle through', *Guardian*, 19 Sep 1985.

Raphael, A., 'MPs Prepare Fudge on Cash Sweetners', *Observer*, 1 Dec 1985.

Rasmussen, J. S., and McCormick, J., 'The Influence of Ideology on British Labour MPs in Voting on EEC Issues', *Legislative Studies*, 10, no. 2 (1985).

Searing, D., 'The Role of the Good Constituency Member and the Practice of Representation in Great Britain', *Journal of Politics*, 47, no. 2 (1985).

Smith, T. A., 'Men of Affairs as Men of Letters', paper presented to the Political Studies Association Conference, 1983.

Summerskill, S., 'Nineteen in the House', *Listener*, 17 Jan 1980.

Vallance, E., 'Women Candidates and Elector Preference', *Politics*, 1, no. (1981).

——, 'Women Candidates in the 1983 General Election', *Parliamentary Affairs*, 37, no. 3 (1984).

——, 'Two Cheers for Equality: Women Candidates in the 1987 Election', *Parliamentary Affairs*, 41, no. 1 (1988).

Index